SPEAK WRIGHT

Sleeping Bear Press
310 North Main
P.O. Box 20
Chelsea, Michigan 48118
www.sleepingbearpress.com

Printed and bound in Canada by Friesens
10 9 8 7 6 5 4 3 2 1

Library of Congress Cataloging-in-Publication Data
Wright, Ben
Speak Wright : A literate guide to the game of golf / by Ben Wright.
p. cm.
ISBN 1-58536-008-2
1. Golf--Terminology. 2. Golf--Miscellanea. I. Title.

GV961.3 .W75 2000
796.352'01'4--dc21

00-009087

SPEAK WRIGHT

A literate guide to the game of golf

Ben Wright

with
Michael Patrick Shiels

Sleeping Bear Press

Introduction

In the four years that I've been exiled from the television broadcast booth, I have watched and listened to hours and hours of televised golf originating from all over the world. Golf is a game that often speaks for itself. Sadly, however, attempts to provide analysis sometimes result in needless and cliché-ridden dialogue.

I've lost count of the times a former touring professional turned announcer has told the audience that the player being observed is 138 yards from the green and needs to hit "a nice nine-iron."

What is a "nice nine-iron"?

Presumably, it means a nine-iron shot that stops within ten or 15 feet of the flagstick. Well, it seems to me that an increasing number of these golf pro/announcers are let loose with a microphone despite the fact that knowledge of the English language, its grammar and its syntax is minimal.

Do major network golf announcers necessarily have to be clichéd shills for the PGA Tour? Perhaps educated writers might be better qualified for the job of describing the beautiful sport of golf. Centuries of playful and literate terms have accompanied the game...some forgotten, some neglected, and some largely unknown.

It was with this in mind that we decided to put together a few words and phrases that might make commentary more colorful for the suffering viewers who, as they have often told me, very often douse the sound during televised golf tournaments. Admittedly some of the suggestions that we have come up with are lighthearted, while others are tongue-in-cheek. Bottom line: it's a gentle potpourri that is meant to be enjoyed, and possibly even used while playing with your weekend morning foursome.

I defer, first, to the late Henry Longhurst, the British golf writer and BBC television announcer who was my guide and mentor. After my first day as an announcer at the Masters in 1973, Longhurst said to me, "We are nothing but caption writers in a picture business. If you can't improve the quality of the pictures with your words, keep your damned mouth shut."

I learned another lesson that same year from my esteemed producer/director at CBS, Frank Chirkinian. Following my use of the American cliché "a whole new ball game" to describe a sudden turn-of-events at the LA Open, Frank shouted at me (only somewhat jokingly), "If I ever understand another word you say, you're fired!" The "Ayatollah," you see (as we announcers called him), wanted me to speak like the Englishman I've always been—not like an American. He wanted me to employ terms that not only were part of the history of the game, but also would provide the colorful paint to illustrate golf with the most literate of language.

Even though the "Ayatollah" had a point back then, we didn't want this book to be a stuffy British dictionary. That's why there are some wonderful American words and phrases included.

As Longhurst—perhaps the finest golf announcer ever—was wont to say, "And there you have it."

Enjoy.

Ben Wright

P.S. Got any great golf terms and phrases that you and your friends use? E-mail them to benwright@sleepingbearpress.com and you just may see them in "SpeakWright II."

A kicking horse

This is an opponent who refuses to be intimidated, worn-down, "ridden," or go gracefully to defeat.

A lot of cabbage

Winnings from a tournament or a big money match.

A mess

In the southern United States, calling someone a "mess" is a high compliment, and it usually means that the person is exciting and the life of the party. "That Skipper Bowles, he's a mess!" is actually praising him when said in a place like South Carolina.

Absolute impenetrability

Refers to a player who is absolutely impervious to challenge. A focused golfer who displays complete and total invincibility. Tiger Woods, for instance, was not to be denied at the 1998 Masters Tournament, just as Ben Hogan was virtually alone in his conquest of Carnoustie at the 1953 Open Championship.

Abundant harvest

A birdie-filled round.

Address

To take aim and prepare to hit the ball. Your address should take no longer than the time it requires you to gather your scattered thoughts before you become a boor.

After lunch

A phrase used to refer to 18 holes played in the afternoon following the morning 18. If you played 36 holes in one day, the second 18 is said to have been after lunch, regardless of whether you actually ate or not.

For instance, at the 1975 Ryder Cup Matches at Laurel Valley Golf Club, Brian Barnes faced Jack Nicklaus in the final days' singles matches. Barnes beat Nicklaus twice in one day, winning an 18-hole match before lunch, and defeating him again after lunch.

After the Lord Mayor's Show

The Lord Mayor's Show in London features a colorful procession of ornate horse-drawn carriages. There are also the unfortunate serfs that follow the horses, shovel in hand, to remove and carry away any horse manure that may have been dropped onto the cobblestone road. The title "mayor" should be pronounced "mare."

In golf, the phrase may be stated with total aplomb on the tee. After the first three golfers in a quartet have hit magnificent long tee shots down the middle. The fourth player must then follow, and it is the joyous responsibility of one of the other players to announce him by trumpeting "after the lord mayor's show" and motioning toward the hitting area.

The very demeaning and wicked phrase is meant to infer that since all of the proud mares have passed through, it is now time for those that shovel manure to follow.

Age of excuses

When the aches, pains and ailments begin to outnumber the

pars, birdies and eagles.

Agonizing stimulus
Watching a consistent opponent play well—hole after hole—is agonizing stimulus.

Agony of indecision
The sometimes difficult and confounding task of choosing between two clubs or two competing strategies. Five-iron or six-iron? Lay up or go for it? Pitch and run, or chip? Hit driver or a safe iron shot down the middle?

Air of antiquity
When a revered golfer of legendary status saunters through a crowd, he gives off an air if antiquity. Byron Nelson, still very active, gives off just such a nostalgic air, as does Sam Snead and other players of an era gone by.

Amateur side
To miss a putt on the "amateur side" is to send the ball rolling below the hole because of the break. This is considered to be an amateur mistake because the ball really never had a chance to even let gravity help it work its way to the cup. Missing a putt on the high side may be said to be missing it on the "professional side" since at least your ball had a chance of breaking and rolling in.

Amidst the peril
When a player suddenly seems surrounded by hazards, dangerous shots, slippery three-putt possibilities, and a hungry

field that's giving chase. The pressure of maintaining a lead in these conditions can be perilous at best.

Apparition of the conqueror
When a great player who is thought to be past his prime shows signs of the brilliance that was once displayed. Good examples are Jack Nicklaus at the 1986 Masters and Johnny Miller at the 1994 AT&T Pebble Beach National Pro-Am.

Apron
This is the ground around a green that specifically leads up the front and through an opening in the fringe to the putting surface. The apron, though, is typically shaved or mowed tightly to allow players to run the ball onto the green.

Aquatic doom
The fate of a sinking golf ball after it has been hit into a water hazard, pond, or burn. During one of my first American television broadcasts, which was the CBS coverage of the Jackie Gleason Inverrary National Airlines Classic in 1973, I described an Arnold Palmer tee shot by saying that it had "plumbed the depths in many acres of aquatic doom." This won me critical acclaim from Miami sportswriter Pete Axthelm...but not much from Arnold.

Arse
A more civilized manner in which to refer to the backside of a fellow or chap. Which reminds me, do not refer to the final nine-holes of a golf layout as the "backside," lest your reference be confused as a description of someone's "arse."

As it lies

Once a ball has been struck from the tee, it must be played as it lies. This may be unfair, such as when the ball lands in a divot, but that is the "rub of the green," which is to say, that is your bad luck. Take your medicine like a big boy, and resist temptation to touch the ball.

It was said of Ben Hogan that during his victorious march around Carnoustie during the 1953 British Open, he played his second shots in the afternoon round from the same divots that he had made in the center of the fairway during his morning round! I know that is rubbish, of course, because Hogan was so good he wouldn't hit his ball into the divots, but rather, right next to them!

Atmospheric tumult

A surprising upset in a match, or a large group of players scoring high numbers due to extreme wind or course conditions.

Augusta National Golf Club

When referring to the site of the Masters Tournament, it is only proper to say the Augusta National Golf Club. Simply sloppily referring to it as Augusta, as so many do, is not only unacceptable, but also plainly inaccurate. Those on the inside actually call it "The National."

Awesome in its power and majesty

This is just about the best way that one can describe an excellent drive. (This phrase should be reserved for only the finest of tee shots.)

Babel clamor of tongues

When a player will accept numerous golf tips and get instruction from anyone, he is lost, because he is hearing a Babel clamor of tongues in an attempt to improve. We all know what happened to the tower of Babel. (It never got built!)

Back side

Never refer to the final nine holes of a golf course as the "back side," because it sounds as if you are referring to someone's bum or arse. The final nine holes may be called the "back nine" or, infinitely more elegant, the "inward half." Since the routing of early golf courses literally took players "out and back" in a loop of holes, the first nine was the "outward half," and after turning around to head for home, the golfers would play the "inward half."

Ball marker

A proper ball marker should be no bigger than a nickel, flat as a dime, and preferably a dull coin. You want the coin to be narrow to allow fellow competitor's putts to roll by unhampered, and as flat as possible so that it will not interfere with the passage of a ball accidentally hit over it. You also want the marker to be dull so that it will not reflect light and shine in an opponent's eyes.

I always liked the plastic ball marker with the little nub on the bottom, but Senior PGA TOUR player and CBS broadcaster Gary McCord admonished me for using them. He claimed that the nub put another spike-mark in the green, and that the use of them was the sign of a true amateur.

I have seen players mark their ball with a huge coin from

some banana republic. Now that's ridiculous!

A dull U.S. penny — is perfect.

Irish Punt — is thin enough and dull to be sure, but way too big.

British Pound — Small enough and dull enough, but too thick.

Canadian Looney — Perfect in color but too big and slightly too thick.

French Franc — Too shiny.

After years of traveling the globe, I prescribe the following coin as the absolute perfect ball marker:

The African Cent — Tiny, dull and thin as a wafer. It's also an attractive coin!

Banana ball
An egregiously sliced ball that bends its way in the shape of a curved banana.

Barber pole
In the United Kingdom especially, flagsticks are striped horizontally using black and white. This aids in spotting the flagsticks through the frequent blowing wind and rain.

You may notice on the Senior PGA TOUR that the flags are checkered yellow and white. This was an idea of Senior TOUR player Bruce Crampton, who was convinced the checkered flags would aid the aging players who may be losing the quality and sharpness of their sight.

Barriers of separation
Rows of trees, hedges, or mounds that divide fairways.

Battlements around the green
A green that is fortified by heavy bunkers or long rough...indeed, battlements not eager to yield par!

Bending from the perpendicular
When a player is picking his ball out of the cup after making a crucial putt.

Bent grass
(See grass.)

Bermuda grass
(See grass.)

Betrayed emotion
When uncontrollable nerves turn treasonous and steal one's confidence and ability. Scott Hoch at The Masters, Doug Sanders at St. Andrews, Greg Norman on a couple of occasions, and nearly all of the PGA TOUR players (at one time or another) have felt the pressure of emotion.

Billows of trouble
A strong but inconsistent wind that tussles the flags and shakes the leaves intermittently.

Bisqe
(pronounced "bisk) This is a stroke deducted at the option of the less skilled player when he sees fit to do so. To explain further: If you are to give your opponent seven strokes at the outset of a match, those seven strokes are normally deducted

from his score at the holes numbered one through seven on the course handicap index. If you're opponent plays one of these seven holes so badly that his even his handicap stroke cannot help affect the result, then he has wasted one of his strokes, and that is a very costly mistake.

The idea of the bisqe is that the inferior player can persuade the better player to give him seven bisqes instead of seven strokes. The inferior player can use one of his seven bisqes after any hole that has been played. This guarantees that the inferior player never wastes any of his handicap strokes. It is a generous game that increases the chances of the underdog to be competitive. This is a traditional British way of doing things.

Bestowing himself in the vacancy
Breaking from the pack to take the lead in a tournament.

Betrayed emotion
When uncontrollable nerves turn treasonous and steal one's confidence and ability. Tom Weiskopf, Scott Hoch, Greg Norman, Doug Sanders, and nearly all of the PGA TOUR players (at one time or another) have felt the pressure of emotion.

Beyond mortal endurance
The greatest and most dramatic of superhuman victories. Ken Venturi's 1964 United States Open Championship at Congressional Country Club in suburban Washington D.C. is perhaps the performance that went furthest beyond mortal endurance. Told that he might not survive the afternoon round of the 36-hole Open final, Venturi braved the oppressive temperatures and struggled through near-fatal heat

exhaustion to finally win his first and only major championship.

Bird of paradise
A very welcome and timely birdie that comes just when it is desperately needed.

Bitter vigor
When a misplayed shot or an ill-timed bogey enrages a player enough to motivate him to play better, he does so with bitter vigor. A player might also compete with bitter vigor against an opponent for which he harbors sincere dislike.

Blind Shot
Facing a blind shot, one must hit the ball without seeing where it is going and without an evident point of aim. Lahinch GC in the west of Ireland, Rye, Royal Cinque Ports at Deal, the Himalayan bunker at St. Enodoc in the village of Rock, Cornwall England, Royal St George's Sandwich Kent, and the seventh hole on the Old Course at St Andrews are perfect examples. With updated earth moving equipment, blind shots are inappropriately absent on modern golf courses and a thing of the past in that respect.

Bloody
Often used in place of the word "damned," but doesn't always need to have a negative connotation. "Bloody good shot," one might say to another player after his tee shot has been soundly struck. "That was my last bloody ball," one might say in disgust as he watches it roll into a burn. If another player in your quartet is lolly-gagging along, you might say to

your fellow competitor, "Get off of your bloody arse and get on the tee."

Blooming bells and balmy fragrance

Wonderful and aesthetically pleasing golf courses featuring flora and fauna.

Blue-assed fly

A fly that buzzes all around in a speedy and frantic fashion in an attempt to warm-up and thaw its frozen backside. During the 1997 Ryder Cup Matches in Sotogrande, Spain, European team captain Seve Ballesteros quickly drove his golf cart around from match to match trying to cheer-on and assist his players. In my opinion, he buzzed around Valderrama GC like a blue-assed fly!

Blunder of a placid intellectual organ

A poor or silly decision sometimes referred to as a "brain cramp."

Broom handle putter

The elongated putter that is stationed against a player's chest or under his chin in a desperate effort to keep from twitching putts.

Bog trotter

A Guinness-swilling, potato-bashing, bog trotter is your average Irishman. It is far better to trot across a peat bog than to sink in one, and the Irish know this very well. If you play golf in Ireland or on an Irish-style course, tread lightly in the rough, or you might never be seen again. Hit your ball too far offline, or venture too far into the rough, and only a "bog trotter" will be able to keep up with you.

Bogey

In the not too distant past, the term "bogey" was actually used to signify "par." Bogey for the course was 72. The word "par," an American creation, was not in golf's original parlance.

A Club Secretary, in an attempt to create a simple scoring system, invented a fictional player named "Colonel Bogey." It was presumed that the imaginary "Colonel Bogey" moved his ball precisely as the course was meant to be played, making a perfect score of "bogey" on each hole. The "Colonel Bogey system" was designed so that fellow competitors might play against each other and all might know how the others were faring.

A score of one under-par was called a "birdie," two under-par was called an "eagle," and a score of three under-par was called an "albatross," which is a very rare bird, and a much more romantic term than "double-eagle," which was a later addition. A score over bogey had no name.

Eventually, standards of play began to improve. American players came to Britain and felt that bogey was realistically one stroke more than players of their skill should need to play the hole properly. They disdained "making a bogey," because they felt they could have done better. Eventually, bogey came to mean a score one-stroke higher than four, and eventually one stroke higher than par.

Boot

The storage area in the rear of an automobile, sometimes unceremoniously referred to as a "trunk" or "deck," is actually called a "boot." Stow your golf clubs in the boot.

Borrowed too much

This means to putt your ball on a line too high for it to take the break and roll in. Conversely, if a player "didn't borrow enough," it means that the ball was not putted with enough break. You may also say that one did not borrow enough on putts that fall short, or that one borrowed too much on putts hit right through the break and past the hole.

Bramble

(See grass.)

Bugger

Since the "granddaddy of all foul words" will never sound appropriate coming from the lips of a learned man, feel free to substitute the word "bugger" in its place. "That bugger could really hit the ball a long way!" You may also employ the word in another conventional use, as when you tell an annoying pest to "bugger off!"

Building a stance

Positioning your feet or body in such a way that you strengthen or fortify your position or balance for the golf swipe. American PGA TOUR player Craig Stadler once put a towel on the ground to protect his pants while hitting a shot from his knees under a tree. He was disqualified for "building an artificial stance." A player may settle his feet firmly and lean against anything, but he may not dig foot holes or put down anything to stand or kneel on.

Stadler, years later, cut the tree down.

Bump and run

Does not exist neither in golf parlance nor in my lexicon. The shot should be called a "chip and run" or "run-up shot." Things go "bump" in the night, and we don't play golf at night. One bumps his head, not his golf ball.

Bungling announcement

Making a poor score on the very first hole.

Bunker

Across the pond, golf courses are covered with cavernous bunkers surrounded with ragged grasses. Sometimes they appear to be crater-like, sand-filled holes. Bunkers should never be referred to as "sand traps," which is a very common mistake. You will not find the term "sand trap" in the Rules of Golf.

Burn

This is the Scottish word for a stream. The Barry Burn is an integral part of the 17th and 18th holes at Carnoustie. The Swilcan Burn is an equally significant feature of the first and 18th holes at the Old Course at St. Andrews.

Burrowing animal

A topped shot that miraculously makes its way to a fairway or green.

Butterfly mind

Incapable of holding concentration through 18 holes, a butterfly mind flits from subject to subject just as a butterfly flits from bush to bush. Gary McCord, for instance, has a brilliant imagination and adequate skills, but his butterfly mind and short attention span prevent him from maintaining and enduring focus on anything. The Senior PGA TOUR is a blessing for McCord, as he now only has to focus for three rounds—one less than they play on the regular tour.

By evil hap

When bad luck occurs during a round, such as your ball rolling into a divot or skipping out of bounds after bouncing off a cart path, it can be said to have occurred by evil hap.

By the scroop

Taking hold of a particular player, match or tournament by the collar, by the scruff, or by the scroop.

Bye

When a player has been beaten before the final hole of a round, a bye is negotiated on the remaining holes. In the way of example, if a player is bested by 6-5, then a new wager would begin through the last five holes. If that bye on those last five holes is won by 3-2, a new match to be played over the remaining two holes is negotiated. This is called a "bye bye."

You may be accustomed to referring to this type of wager as a "press," but it actually is called a bye.

Cabbage

An acceptable and colorful universal term to describe thick rough.

Calamitous result

This is a poor outcome in a match. If a better player is defeated in an upset, this is a calamitous result. If a player of equal skill is thrashed in a merciless rout, it is a calamitous result.

Canary

This is a player who talks too much on the golf course, chirping and singing the praises of every shot hit, recounting his holes, and overanalyzing his swing and the swings of others. As Frank Sinatra used to say, "Pray, silence."

Car park

Seve Ballesteros played a shot from the car park adjacent to the 16th fairway at Royal Lytham Golf Club on the way to winning his first Open Championship. He did not, you'll note, play from something called a "parking lot." Try to use the term car park, and hope you don't have to play from one!

Carry

The word "carry" can be used as a noun or a verb. Your shot must carry the water or the ball must carry a bunker, which is to fly over. When sizing up a dangerous shot over water and the yardage needed to successfully execute the play, one might say "the 'carry' here is 210 yards."

Of course, if you have a weak partner in a fourball, you may have to play better just to "carry" your team and your partner through the match.

Cartloads of yen
What Graham Marsh won playing on the Japanese Tour during his long and illustrious career.

Cartpathian
A golf shot that bounces off of the cart path, resulting in a high hop and an out of control ball, is a cartpathian shot.

Casual untidiness
Wastefully missing a short putt by hurrying or not giving the game the constant attention it demands. When a player carelessly lets an opponent get back into a match when he was nearly eliminated, the player is also guilty of casual untidiness.

Casual water
When soaking water outside of the hazards comes up over the welts of your shoes, it is said by the rules to be casual water. Welts are soles and heels, and if the water reaches the body of the shoe, the player is allowed relief. Before a player can take relief, he must demonstrate that he needs it by raising water with his feet while walking naturally. While playing in England they may be sorely needed, but flippers may not be worn for this purpose.

Cat box
Slang name for a bunker.

Champion

The winner of a true championship tournament. The PGA Championship, the Open Championship, the United States Open Golf Championship, the British Amateur Championship, the TOUR Championship, the Cliffs Valley Club Championship, and so forth.

Charitable establishment

The PGA TOUR, for both the players and the cities where its tournaments are held.

Check-up

A ball that hits the green and stops quickly is one that has checked-up.

Chill of despair invading his heart

The almost visible expression on the face of a player losing his confidence during a round.

Chink in the armor

An opponent's sign of weakness is the chink in his armor. A fear or worry, or an area of poor skill can be a chink in your armor as well. If you do not fancy the run-up shot or are, perhaps, incapable of hitting an effective flop shot, then you have identified your chink in the armor. When faced with that type of shot, your misplay will reveal this chink to your opponent.

Choking

This is a horrible term that is often applied to a fellow competitor (or yourself) who has apparently snatched defeat from the jaws of victory. Better and kinder to say that someone is "falling apart at the seams" or that "the wheels are coming off."

Chord of sympathy

A knowing shrug from your fellow competitor when things aren't going well for you on the golf course.

Chummed about

Refers to spending time with one's friends or chums. Dropping in on a pub after the round to recount your match, driving out to a golf game, or traveling on a golf vacation are ways that fellows might chum about.

Since there weren't many British journalists in Chaska, Minnesota to cover the 1970 United States Open Championship at Hazeltine National GC, I chummed about all week with eventual winner Tony Jacklin, who was happy to have the company of a fellow Brit so far from home.

Cinderella story

This is a cliché way to characterize a surprising and popular success. Sometimes a cliché is justifiable, and I happen to rather like this one. When a player has watched his pumpkin of a game turn into a gilded coach that takes him from rags to riches, only a cliché will do!

Circumstances of demand

Tough competition or difficult weather conditions on the golf course.

Circumventing nature

A shot that seems to defy all logistical and geographic sense. When a shot rattles around in the trees and is then tossed back out into the fairway, the ball apparently circumvented nature. A ball might also circumvent nature by skipping across a pond or threading its way though heavy forestry.

Classic

The attachment of the word classic to the title of a tournament is despicable and totally unnecessary. Very often, these so-called classics are not worthy of the name. The Bob Hope Desert Classic is named after a comedian for god's sake! The definition of classic is an event of first class, acknowledged excellence, which usually cannot aptly be determined until after it happens. The competition may have been classic. The ending may have been classic. There may have been certain goings-on that could be considered classic. However, it is presumptuous of anyone to call his own event a classic in advance or after.

Clergyman's stipend

A meager amount of payment or winnings. (See Cooley Wages.)

Cliff

A cliff features ledges and, unlike a precipice, has vegetation such that it might be hard to go over, and craggy edges that extend out and might break your fall or actually be scaleable. The 16th hole at Torrey Pines South Course in La Jolla, California runs along a cliff. If you venture far enough to peer over the side, you might be rewarded with—or perhaps appalled at—

the sight of revelers skinny dipping in the ocean below.

Cloak of gray freeze

When a player becomes overwhelmed with frustration and
inability to play, he is said to be "cloaked with gray freeze."
His mind is unable to focus and he finds himself missing
greens and fairways and yipping putts.

Cloud of bewilderment

When a player settles into a series of bad shots or poor holes, he
will feel as if he has disappeared into a cloud of bewilderment.

Clubhouse

The main building at a golf course. It often contains dining
facilities and changing. In the United Kingdom, you might
encounter a guest locker room if you are fortunate. But beware,
because you are not always welcome into the main clubhouse.
You might be offered the use of a changing room without
lockers. Royal Troon, Portmarnock, and Royal County Down,
for instance, even go so far as to have separate dining facilities
for guests. Guest dining facilities and changing areas are typically more frugal and more pedestrian than the member facilities. Do not get your feelings hurt, however, because mem-
bership must have its privileges.

Clubs

Here are a few of the ancient and proper names for golf clubs:

Brassie

Is a 2-wood type club used for attaining maximum

distance off of the turf with a low trajectory.

Cleek
A long-shafted iron for lengthy and low shots. The cleek is equivalent to the modern 1-iron.

Driver
Virtually identical to the modern equivalent, and used for the same purpose.

Driving Mashie
A long-shafted, slightly lofted club for driving the ball from the tee. The driving mashie really has no modern equivalent.

Jigger
A shallow-faced, all purpose chipping club. I suppose its modern equivalent might be the trouble clubs or putter-like chipping clubs that have surfaced on the market.

Mashie Niblick
The equivalent of a modern 7-iron.

Mid-Iron
The equivalent of a modern 3-Iron.

Mongrel Mashie
The equivalent of a modern 4-iron.

Niblick
The equivalent of the modern 8- and 9-irons.

Ordinary Mashie
The equivalent of a modern 5-iron.

Spade Mashie
With a deep face, the spade mashie is the equivalent of a modern 6-iron.

Spoon
The equivalent of a modern 3-wood.

Cocking a snook
When the erratic layout of a golf course turns away from the out-then-in pattern of links, it is said to be cocking a snook. At the Old Course at St. Andrews, the eighth hole ("Short") and ninth hole ("End") cock a snook back toward the clubhouse before heading back out and completing the loop.

Come back!
This plaintive wail—desperate in nature—pleads with the laws of physics to cease long enough to save a wayward shot and prevent it from soaring into woods, water or out-of-bounds.

Commencement of spring
For many golf enthusiasts, spring does not begin until Byron Nelson and Sam Snead belt their honorary tee shots down the first fairway of the Augusta National Golf Club to open The Masters tournament each April.

Compelled perforce to accept defeat

This is the act of facing the inevitable loss at the hands of a player who is dominating a match or stroke play tournament.

Compellingly dramatic

This is a match or a competition that is so exciting that one's attention is totally commanded by it.

Congealed relics of autumn

Refers to a golfer's clubs that have been put away for the season.

Conviction of observation

When a player of sound course management skills surveys a hole and devises his strategy with determination. This term might also be applied to the reading of a tricky putt.

Coolie wages

Refers to very poor, low wages. Many, many years ago, a coolie was a servant to the English in India when that country was ruled by the British Empire.

When you win a small wager on the golf course, you might say that you had to "play awfully hard for these coolie wages" when you are being paid.

Corroborating the surmise

Winning when expected to.

Country club

A club that not only features a golf course, but also chooses to offer tennis courts, a swimming pool, and social events.

(See golf club.)

Crossing the palm with silver

When a golfer is forced to hand over the money to pay off a bet that he's lost.

Crowning brutality

This is the act of denying any small measure of satisfaction to an opponent by adding superfluous birdies to win by a wide margin or, in a match, conquering with a significant number of holes to play.

Cudgel

This is another colorful name for a golf club carried around by a player. (See Pilgrim's staff.)

Customer golf

Sometimes called "client golf." It is the underhanded act of selling-out and contriving to narrowly lose a golf match to a potential customer in the hope of doing business with them. Clients also tend to have an advantage when playing with those who would hope to increase their business involvement or maintain their business relationship.

When I think of those who submit themselves to purposely losing in a round of customer golf, it reminds me of the old saying: "Now that we've established what you are, we merely have to determine your price."

Cut

Hitting a cut-shot is to hit a ball in a way that will make it turn from the left-to-right—either off the tee or toward a green. I have found, however, that if a shot is poorly aimed and headed way to the left, a player will audibly plead for the ball to "cut!" in an attempt to convince the players in his group that he did it on purpose.

Cut is a real ruse of a word that can make anyone appear to be a skilled player.

Daily fee golf course

This is a term that has come into use of late to designate golf courses with no members but of private club quality. In other words, you can gain the privileges of a member by paying a "daily fee" instead of an initiation fee and monthly dues.

I don't support the need for a term like "daily fee." In my opinion, golf courses are private, semi-private, public or municipal. Daily fee seems to be an effort to remove the perceived class distinction between public and private golfer, but, after all, they are two different segments of golfers. There is no shame in either.

Daylight stroke

A very short, very quick putting stroke. As soon as a player sees "daylight" between the putter and ball on the takeaway, he moves the putter forward and jabs at the ball.

Deadly soporific

One who lulls his opponent to sleep with very deliberate (slow) play. The style may be uninspiring and unremarkable, but it can drain the life from an opponent just as easily.

Deep-branded in the memory

This refers to an unforgettable experience, positive or negative, which a player can draw upon or be haunted by. Greg Norman's dark experience at The Masters in 1996 is surely deep-branded in his psyche.

Descending the steps

This refers to climbing down into a deep pot bunker or—

unfortunately—climbing down a leaderboard.

Desolate wanderer
This describes a TOUR member who hops from event to event in hopes of making a cut and some measure of a paycheck, though never, ever threatening to win.

Detestable substitute
A second-place finish.

Dew sweepers
This is the first group of players on a golf course on a given day. They are usually out early enough to putt and play their balls through the same dew on which they must tread. In tournament play, these competitors are at or near the back of the pack and many strokes off the lead.

Disrelish for the occupation
Describes a professional player who would seem to desire to be anywhere but on the golf course. Perhaps his game has gone bad, or perhaps his disrelish for the occupation is promoted by the fact that he cannot handle the stress. A player who has trouble mercilessly disposing of an opponent might also seem to harbor some disrelish for the occupation.

This could also apply to Byron Nelson who quit competitive golf to run his ranch in Texas that he bought with his winnings.

Do not overwork the ox that grinds your corn
Bob Ferrier, during his career as a sportswriter, was sent to

cover World Cup soccer in Chile. Finally arriving at his hotel, Ferrier received word from his sports editor back in London, asking him if he would travel up-country to cover a warm-up match the English team was going to play. Ferrier knew that this was a very insignificant game, and didn't feel that he should be asked to go into the wilds to cover it. In response, therefore, Ferrier sent a cable back to his sports editor with his response. It read simply "Do not overwork the ox that grinds your corn."

When your partner is not playing very well and you are left to carry him though a match, you might like to pour scorn on him by warning him: "Do not overwork the ox that grinds your corn."

Try saying it to your boss sometime, as well. You'll probably end up with more time to play golf...and no paycheck to settle your fees with!

Doctrine of endurance
The uncanny ability to struggle mightily against an opponent and not surrender no matter what pace he sets.

Doctrines of nature
The undeniable law of the jungle on the PGA TOUR. Winning is difficult, and it is even more difficult to learn to learn how to win. Patience coupled with tenacity and a dash of seasoning is typically a doctrine of nature.

Dogleg
When one cannot see a green from the tee because the fairway turns to the right or left, the hole may be referred to as a

"dogleg." No particular type of dog specified. In the case of a dogleg, any old mongrel will do.

In a rebellious show of contempt cleverly disguised as respect, I once named a canine pet of mine "Frank," after my stern producer/director at CBS, Frank Chirkinian. Chirkinian, who imagined that I took out my frustrations by pouring scorn on that poor beast, acquired his own pet and gave the dog the namesake, "Bentley."

Dog's license

In the old days, if you lost a match by seven & six (7-6), you were said to have been "given your dog's license."

In Britain, the cost of a dog's license was seven shillings and six pence. I remember beating my father by 7-6 when I was a young, up-and-coming player. I went home and bragged that I'd handed him his dog license. He was so offended that he said he would nevermore play golf with me.

Donkey's years

This is an old expression that means a very, very long time. If slow play has caused you to experience a very long round, you might exclaim, "We were out there for donkey's years!" Or, during a slump, one might complain, "I haven't broken 80 in donkey's years!"

Donkeys, you see, live to be very old.

Dormie

The term dormie can only be used in a match that is to end at the 18th or 36th hole without a playoff or extra holes. When a player's match is dormie, it means that he cannot lose.

For instance, a player might be "dormie four." This means that he is four holes up with four holes to play. Therefore, even if the player were to lose the last four holes, he can get no worse than a half.

Double or quits
This is the proper British way to call for a bet of "double or nothing."

Dour of countenance
Means stone-faced and grumpy. There was nothing light-hearted about Ben Hogan, who frequently appeared grim and dour of countenance. This appearance often intimidated and down-right frightened his opponents.

Drawing breath
Heavy breathing down the stretch due to nervousness or lack of experience. Ken Venturi, my former colleague at CBS and one-time United States Open Champion, insists that if you don't get nervous down the stretch, you shouldn't be playing. It's the excitement of a head-to-head battle that makes it all worthwhile.

Dreaded pond
Any water hazard is to be dreaded. "Devlin's Billabong" on the Torrey Pines South Course is infamous, as is the pond that fronts the 18th hole on the Blue Monster course at the Doral Resort and Spa. If he did not dread it before, Jean Van de Velde certainly now must dread the Barrie Burn at Carnoustie as much as Jack Lemon dreads the Pacific Ocean

along the 18th hole at Pebble Beach.

Dree and dreary
A poor display of golf skills.

Drink himself legless
When a post-round celebration at the 19th hole goes on too long, one of the revelers might imbibe beyond his limit and drink himself legless, such that he is literally unable to walk due to intoxication.

Drubbing
This refers to a merciless victory by figuratively beating, thrashing, and spanking one's opponent.

Duff
This is one way to describe a poorly hit, ugly, horrid, scurrying, ineffectual stroke. The ball can be duffed off the tee, down the fairway—anywhere.

Duffer
This is a popular description of a golfer who has proven himself to be incompetent by relentless, terrible attempts and endless effort. A beginner does not qualify as a duffer, because a beginner at least has potential. A duffer merrily plugs along, gleefully oblivious to his ineptitude, perhaps believing that success and glory are due at any moment.

Durable as flint
Tough, grinding players like Raymond Floyd, Payne Stewart,

and Curtis Strange, who were not great players initially but had durable games that became suitable to win extremely difficult Championships like the U.S. Open.

Elegant diversion

Golf, by its purest of definitions.

Eluding observation

When a player, not among the final pairings, shoots a low score in the last round and vaults himself to unexpected victory, he has done so while eluding observation. This causes havoc to the TV network covering the event because the conclusion might be settled long before the telecast begins

Embers of decaying ability

When a very good player can no longer play to the high standards he once set, but can only occasionally display the fiery talent with which he once toasted opponents.

Entering the land of slumber

When a player begins to slip into a somnolent display of golf that yields poor scores, he in rapidly descending into golf course sleep walking.

Escarpment

This describes more of a gentle slope than a precipice, and generally not as high, but still a steep slope at the edge of a plateau. The Tournament Players Club at Avenel features an escarpment that borders the 13th with a creek below.

Eschscholtzia

(See "grass.")

Estranged relative
When a golfer plays a number of holes without a good score. His relationship to birdie and par becomes as strained as the former marriage of Donald Trump and his latest former girlfriend.

Etiquette
The true definition of golf etiquette is consideration such that you would appreciate people to extend toward you. The interesting thing about golf etiquette is that players cannot be punished for breaching it, which, I feel, is a tragedy. You should do as you'd be done by.

Bad behavior is the most problematic part of the game right now, particularly as the sport explodes in popularity and is thrust upon the masses. Nobody seems to be bothering with manners and tradition. In a most evident example, even fanatically private clubs find pitch marks left all over the greens by players who think they are too important to repair them. The Rules of Golf say "you must" in regards to playing procedure, but only "you should" in the delicate area of etiquette.

Even a stopped clock is correct twice a day
An expression of British origin that may be used as a backhanded compliment to a fellow competitor who executes a good shot during a round full of mediocre ones. Like the clock, the players' hands were finally in the right place, and he somehow found the proper timing. He must have made good contact with the face, and the result alarmed the rest of the group. Please be careful when using puns like this one, because it can trigger an avalanche of bad ones to follow, as I have just

exhibited. The American equivalent is: "Even a blind squirrel finds an acorn every once in a while."

Evil little poltroon

This is an unsporting fellow who either refuses to accept a golf wager, or else insists on negotiating it to the point that it is sided to his favor.

The examination

The sport of golf can be referred to as "the examination." Length off the tee, concentration, short game skills, and stamina are a few of the many aspects of the examination.

Excellent benefactor

This is one way to describe a great partner. A player of fine ability or generous handicap who assists greatly in the winning of a match.

Extinguishing the candle

Finishing off an opponent by dousing what little flame of hope he had burning.

Failing with monotonous regularity

When players hit a mid-round slump, sometimes it is referred to as "having the wheels come off." Failing with monotonous regularity is a haughtier and more British way to describe such a woeful scene.

Far off fire

The sounds of applauding galleries echoing from other fairways and greens, indicating that another player might be making a charge.

Fear of infection

This fear causes otherwise non-superstitious players to look away when a fellow competitor is having a rough go of it with an unrecognizable swing. Nobody wants to get the "shanks" by watching someone else suffer through them, nor do they desire to subconsciously incorporate bad swing habits into their own through the auto-suggestion caused by witnessing a poor swing.

Fescue

(See "grass.")

Feverish with labor

A golfer who is determined to win or play well. Totally focused on the game at hand or the importance of practice. Gary Player spent his career working in this manner.

F.I.D.O.

When a player's score on a given hole begins to rise past the level of double-bogey, someone in the group should mutter the word, "Fido." It's an acronym meaning, "Forget it, drive on."

Flagstick
This is the only acceptable way to refer to the stick that protrudes up from, and reveals the location of, the cup. Despite the pervasive use of the term "pin," a "pin" is something that you use to keep your pants from falling down. The word pin has no place on the golf course. A player should aim for the flagstick not the pin, and study the cup locations not the pin placements.

Flatter father's handicap
An easy golf course can be said to be one that flatters father's handicap.

Flea in your ear, and a foot in your rear
This is an accusatory British expression of sharp reproof, rebuke, or pointed blame. It's appropriate to use this expression when your partner makes a foolish mistake.

Flier
A hot shot caused by grass getting trapped between the ball and the clubface. The ball then flies wildly and uncontrollably, often soaring over the green or perhaps out of play.

Foozle
To foozle a shot is to miss the ball so badly that it only travels a few yards.

For export

When your match is getting tight and it looks as though you might lose a wager to your opponent, the money in your pocket would seem to be "for export."

When it looked as though Bernhard Langer would beat Chip Beck in the 1993 Masters Tournament and become the fifth foreign winner in six years, I said on the CBS telecast that, "It looks like the green jacket is once again for export."

Forced to take an early bath

The loser of a match that does not get close to going the full 18 holes is said to have been sent from the course by being forced to take an early bath.

Forlorn hope

When European Ryder Cup Captain Mark James sent Jean Van de Velde out early in the singles lineup on the final day of the 1999 Matches at Brookline, the Frenchman surely must have experienced forlorn hope. Van de Velde was a sacrificial lamb, in a sense, since United States Captain Ben Crenshaw, with his team trailing desperately, was sure to stack the top of his order with his best players. Since James hadn't played Van de Velde at all during the first two days, he would make his first Ryder Cup appearance in a singles match against America's best...with forlorn hope.

Fortnight

Two weeks.

Fraught with danger
A challenging hole or difficult golf course.

Fringe
This is the tight circle of grass, varying in length, which surrounds and gives definition to the putting surface. Players who miss the green to the right or left must contend with the fringe, and perhaps hit or putt their ball from it.

I abhor the frequent use of the word "collar" to refer to this area around the green. The word collar immediately brings to mind the thought of choking!

Furlong
An eighth of a mile or 220 yards, which makes for a long par-three.

Gaiety of desertion

Winning one's way off of the Buy.com Tour, formerly the Nike Tour, formerly the Hogan Tour, in order to play on the PGA TOUR.

Gandian patience

A decidedly British way to refer to the "patience of Job." The Indian objector was difficult for the British to deal with because he simply would not back down or be denied in his effort to accomplish his beliefs. Good things are bound to happen for a golfer who can maintain this kind of even, deliberate patience.

Ganzy

A perfectly flashy slang word that designates a sweater and warm covering that one might wear over a golf shirt. Tom Weiskopf wore a somewhat less than appealing purple ganzy during his final-round run at the 1975 Masters Tournament. In hindsight, it is probably a good thing he didn't win because the green jacket would have been a pitiful clash with a purple ganzy.

Garden of Eden

The ideal position in a fairway from which to approach a green.

Germs of indignation

This refers to the beginning of a slight annoyance at an opponent.

Getting pissed on

When rain interrupts a round.

Ghastly wakefulness

The sudden realization that a match is destined to be lost, or that the amount of time for a comeback in a round or tournament is running short.

Gimmie

This is the American expression that means a conceded putt. You might be surprised to know that I do believe in gimmies—during casual rounds. A few inches are no bother, and conceding a putt of that insignificant length is common decent manners, and helps to speed up the game. During tournaments, however, you should putt out everything.

Ginty

A club with a V-shaped sole designed to cut through deep rough. The Ginty was a forerunner of the 5-wood and some of the other lofted woods and trouble clubs (Railer, Heaven Wood, etc.).

Give way

This means to allow the group of golfers following you to "play through." Golfers should always give way to speedier players or groups with a lesser number of players than your own.

Goat ranch

An untidy golf course.

Goblin-like

The best way to describe Ian Woosnam.

Golf buggy

This is a motorized golf cart. Golf buggies, increasingly per-vasive in the United States, have been the ruination of many a physique. I was a thin person when I came to America, and the often-mandatory use of the golf buggy has made me a fat person. Paved paths to accommodate the buggies are an unwel-come encroachment on the game as well.

Golf club

Distinctly different than a "country club" in that it features golf...and golf only. Do not go there to play tennis, swim, or attend a society event, because none of those pursuits are offered or available. (See country club)

Golf shoes

Do not lazily refer to golf shoes as spikes or cleats. Style and color may be of your own fortunate or unfortunate choosing. Just please remember not to move your golf shoes when another player is at address. It might distract him.

Golf shop

The same as a professional's shop, which is imminently prefer-able—especially at a famous club.

Golf widow

A wife (or a husband for that matter) left behind while the spouse endeavors to play the game.

Got tight

To say that a shot "got tight" when one actually means to

say that it was hit close to the cup is a mistake. To say that a fellow got tight really means that he got drunk. Saying, rather, that the ball snuggled up to the hole or the flagstick is a much more sober way to refer to a good shot.

Grass

British- and Scottish-style courses have become very popular among American players. The different, yet very distinct features of the courses vary greatly, and an effort should be made to properly refer to each type of hazard, characteristic or grass.

Bentgrass

Exceptionally fine grass that cannot exist in hot weather locales. Bent grass is preferred for putting surfaces, since it has less grain and allows for better roll.

Bermudagrass

A good surface for hot weather locations. Bermuda grass, with course blades, goes brown and dormant in the winter.

Bramble

A prickly shrub on which wild fruit grows. Fleshy blackberries, wild raspberries signify bramble.

Eschscholtzia

A yellow, flowering, Californian Poppy. It is also the only word I have ever spelled incorrectly in a spelling bee. It is pronounced "Es-coal-zee-yah," and the correct employment of this word will make you sound like either a golf course expert or a genuine naturalist.

Fescue

Is found often in pastures. Hay and fescue are frequently and mistakenly referred to as heather.

Gorse

A bush of scrofulous proportions that can literally tear a player limb from limb. The piercing spines of gorse are only beautiful to the beholder in the month of June, when it produces gorgeous yellow flowers. Do not be fooled, though; this beauty is a beast that is impossible and even dangerous to try to hit a ball from. Don't go near its spiny reaches, and don't even try to back into it unless you favor a sore bum. Gorse bushes can grow to be as tall as ten feet high, as they do at Royal County Down Golf Club in Northern Ireland, and on various European wastelands.

Hay

The proper term for indigenous fescue that grows to wildly monumental proportions. It is very difficult to find your ball if you hit it into the hay, where it can virtually sit down and hide.

Heather

A groundcover-type shrub that should be allowed to get high. Wiry stems topped with purple flowers make heather easily recognizable, as the words of the Scottish song that speaks of the "bonnie purple heather."

Heather grows especially on Moors and Heaths.

Kentucky Bluegrass

PGA TOUR players told the Western Golf Association that they didn't want to play in the Western Open if Butler National Golf Club, the tournament's site, didn't do away with Blue Grass fairways. Golfers got fliers out of Blue Grass, and Butler National made the change to bent grass. Blue Grass rough is miserable to play out of.

Kikuyu

A grass indigenous to South Africa. There was a Kikuyu Tribe that perpetrated the demise of the British who had colonized Kenya before its independence. The grass named for the tribe now perpetrates the demise of many members of Riviera Country Club in Los Angeles. The site of the Nissan Open features patches of Kikuyu grass rough that is like barbed wire. Keep out of it at all costs, since your club can be fruitlessly tangled in it and an iron can cut right under a ball perched in Kikuyu grass.

Some golf courses, such as the Gary Player course at Sun City in Africa's Northwest Territory, are covered entirely in Kikuyu, which is amazingly wonderful to play off of when it is trimmed.

Willow Scrub

A low-lying, villainous bush with a horrendous spine and orange, berry-type flowers. It is vegetation composed of brushwood and stunted forest growth. Willow Scrubs inhabit the golf course at Royal Birkdale.

Zoysiagrass
The Tournament Players Club at Avenel was created entirely with Zoysia, and it is beautiful when it is trimmed. When it makes up the rough, though, it becomes spongy and it gobbles up balls. You cannot run the ball on Zoysia.

Grave Diggers' Arms
Strong, thick, developed forearms. I used this phrase on the air at CBS to describe the forearms of Arnold Palmer and later, Tom Watson, both of whom had the very well muscled, bulging arms that a gravedigger might develop from all of his grim digging and shoveling.

Great book
When a player has put together four sub-par rounds in a tournament, he's written himself a great book.

Habitual mood of success

When a player gets his game on a roll and seems to hit every shot perfectly and make every putt, he can be said to be in a habitual mood of success.

Habitually obedient

When the golf ball repeatedly lands in the fairway and settles on the green where one wishes it to, you might remark with amazement that the ball seems habitually obedient.

Hacker

This is a bad golfer who will always be a poor golfer. He will never get any better, and is content merely to hack the ball around in the same poor manner. A hacker unashamedly doesn't practice, and is not the least bit inclined to receive instruction or take any action to better his skills.

Had a couple of sherbets

Drank a few cocktails in the clubhouse bar.

Half

In match play, a score that is the same as one's opponent on a given hole. You can earn a half on a hole by tying your partner. You might be left with a three-foot putt for a half. It is important to remember that half is a noun.

Half pint

A small ale...or PGA TOUR member Jeff Sluman.

Halve

To divide into two parts and share equally. If you have made the same score as your opponent on a given hole in match play, then you have halved the hole. You may also halve the match. It is important to remember that halve is a verb. Players sometimes confuse the use of the words half and halve.

Hand on heart

To infer honesty. "Hand on heart my handicap index is 18," one might say when trying to convince a prospective opponent that you are sincere.

Harmony of squareness

Hitting a ball perfectly on the sweet spot and straight.

Have a dash at it

This means to "go for it." To boldly attempt to pull off a tough shot or beat a better opponent.

He didn't leave anything behind in his shoes

This means a player who has hit a lengthy drive after calling upon every ounce of his strength. "He didn't spare anything there," is the way I once described a drive by Seve Ballesteros after the CBS camera showed him taking a huge cut at it off of the tee.

Headed

When a player never loses the lead in a match or tournament, he has never been headed. No other players got ahead of him.

Heap of dead rabbits
The group of PGA TOUR players who won't make cut and will have to clean out their lockers and leave town early. Typically, they will rabbit (move on) to the next event, packing a corporate appearance or pro-am in between.

Heath
An area of flat, uncultivated land with low shrubs. Walton Heath Golf Club, and Royal Blackheath Golf Club are examples of Heathland-type golf courses.

Hello
This is a simple expression that CBS golf analyst Ken Venturi would sometimes use to punctuate the falling of a putt into the hole.

Hole high
If your ball is hole high, it has come to rest to the right or left of the flagstick but not as close as you had hoped. Please do not use the phrase "pin high." (See "flagstick")

Holing out
Properly spoken, a player "holes a putt," and he "holes out" a golf ball. One does not "hole out" a putt, nor does one "hole" a golf ball.

Home hole
This is the very British way to refer to the 18th and final hole of a golf course.

Honor

What the person who plays first from any given tee has. The honor is always awarded based on the previous gross score rather than the net score. In match play, it is the right of driving off first for having won the preceding hole.

Horse

I have played in many charity fundraising "scramble" tournaments. Often, I have heard the superior player of these four and five-player teams referred to as "the horse." The best player should not be called a horse, but rather should be referred to as the "A player." My skills will never allow me to be referred to as the horse or the A player, but I think a player with such significant skill should be afforded at least a little respect while he carries his partners.

Hospital swing

A very weak pass at the ball.

Hummocks

This is a raised area along the ground. Also called a hillock or hammock.

Hung the moon

When one greatly admires another player or person, he is said to feel that the person "hung the moon." For example, Ken Venturi is a great admirer of Byron Nelson. He thinks Nelson "hung the moon."

Hurried in gait and action

A fast, speedy player—sometimes to his disadvantage.

Hurried-out prayers

When the fate of a golf ball in flight is in doubt, one would be surprised at how quickly pleas of worship can be uttered.

I caught a cold with that one

Exclamation made after an attempted shot has gone awry or a business deal has failed. If you joined your partner in a major wager and then lost the match, you could say you caught a cold with that arrangement.

Idiot's lantern

A television set, or, in these modern days, a laptop computer. If cellular telephones and pagers aren't bad enough, I have literally seen online traders and investors toting their computers around on their golf buggies, checking the market and sending e-mail in the middle of a match! The sight is abhorrent!

Ignominious and abrupt dismissal

The swift, decisive, and unfavorable ending of a match.

Imparted strength

When a player gets a tip from his partner or takes motivation and inspiration from another player in the group, it can be said that he is competing on imparted strength.

Imperial dignity

Bobby Jones, Ben Hogan, and Jack Nicklaus were able to carry themselves in a most imperious manner. By contrast, a player like Arnold Palmer, though he had dignity, really was more a man of the people than a deity. Gary Player was the consummate gritty underdog, and Tiger Woods displays a sometimes petulant, sometimes enthusiastic youthfulness.

Impudence too shameful for remark
This is a mistake that's so bad that it is not only hard to watch, but impossible to comment on. Fellow competitors turn away with embarrassment, pretending not to have seen it.

In a sea of billow and spray
When the waves crash onto a golf course that is immediately adjacent to a mighty ocean, the players and course could be shrouded in a sea of billow and spray.

   This is possible at golf courses like Cypress Point, Ballybunion, and Pebble Beach.

In the pocket
When a four-ball partner ceases playing a hole because it is clear that his score cannot factor into the result of the hole, he is said to be "in the pocket" because that's where his ball should be.

In the shade
A ball hit significantly off to one side of the fairway.

Inestimable damage
A resounding beating such that the depth of the embarrassment to the losers' ego cannot be immediately gauged. The defeat and the shattering of confidence could have an echoing effect on the loser.

Inferiority of description
The mindless chatter of some golf announcers when given the charge of describing the play of the finest golfers in the world

at the peak of their competitive careers.

Inflection

Though proper use of the English language might sound a little odd coming from your mouth, try not to be embarrassed. Though you are not British, it is perfectly appropriate for you to unabashedly employ British affectations in your speech, no matter how pompous it seems to make you sound. You don't need a license, and you don't need to have been born in the United Kingdom or even a Commonwealth.

For instance, Americans typically pronounce the name Bernhard as "Buhr-nahrd," with the emphasis on the second syllable. The British would say "Burn-erd," with the emphasis on the first syllable. Try it!

Similarly, the Americans typically pronounce the name of the originally British luxury motor car by saying "Jag-wahr," with the emphasis on the first syllable. The British rather dramatically pronounce the word "Jag-you-are," with the emphasis on the middle syllable.

Once you get used to this change in dialect, you'll have no trouble.

Inhabited by victories

A season loaded with wins. Byron Nelson's 1945 season, with 18 wins, could only be described as being inhabited by victories. Sam Snead's 1950 season was inhabited by 11 victories. Tiger Woods' 1999 year of eight wins was a season inhabited by victories.

Inside the leather

A putt that measures less than the length of the shaft of a putter, excluding the leather grip. In friendly matches, putts of this length are considered to be "good" (conceded) and are never actually measured.

Instinctive certainty

The self-assurance of a superior, more experienced player in facing a rookie or younger golfer. Confidence on the golf course and in competition.

Insupportable oppression

The merciless defeat of a player through lucky shots, unlikely long putts, and holed bunker shots is a display of insupportable oppression. Greg Norman suffered insupportable oppression by losing more than a few tournaments through the insupportable oppression of players such as Larry Mize at the 1987 Masters Tournament and Bob Tway at the 1986 PGA Championship. Mize chipped-in after missing the green in the sudden death playoff, and Tway holed-out a bunker shot on the last hole of the championship.

Interloper

A flash in the pan player; a pretender; one who tries to act as if he belongs. It might be said, on a larger scale, that Gary McCord was an interloper on the PGA TOUR.

It is in the lap of the gods

A splendid saying to employ when only fate can truly decide

the outcome of a shot or a match. When Fred Couples hit his tee shot onto the steep and shaved bank that fronts the 12th green at the Augusta National Golf Club during the final round of the Masters in 1992, it was "in the lap of the gods" as to whether the ball would stay up or roll back into Rae's Creek. It stayed up. Therefore, his victory, too, was "in the lap of the gods."

Whether I break 80 in my next competitive round is "in the lap of the gods."

If you beat your boss in a round of golf, the status of your employment may be "in the lap of the gods."

Italian bandit
Constantino Rocca, the appealing and popular player from Italy, whose unconventional swing has won him more than his fair share of earnings, and nearly led him to Masters and Open Championship victories.

It's not over 'till the green hits the bottom of the bucket
I believe it was Damon Runyon who coined this phrase, but it seems to fit in the high stakes, competitive world of professional golf.

Jam on the anchor
Stepping on the brakes of one's motorized golf cart, or any automobile.

Jar
I've heard the hole or cup referred to as "the jar," but jar is more commonly known in Ireland to be a glass of whiskey. When the Irish tell you that a fellow is "fond of the jar," they mean that he likes to drink.

Jealous guardianship
A player who is protecting a lead or defending a title might do so with a spirit of jealous guardianship.

Joe Bloggs
The British name for the average Joe that Americans know as "Joe Blow" or "Joe Lunch bucket." He's your average municipal golf course player.

Jungle
Treacherous undergrowth that has many colorful names, including "spinach," "cabbage," "trouble," and "hay." But please don't use "schmoogies," "gunk," or anything that sounds tacky like that.

Junket
Is not a golf trip, but rather is a British dessert. It is a sort of a blancmang. I suspect you're none the wiser now. Junket, or blancmang is a dish of sweetened and flavored curds, often served with fruit or cream. It is a sweet, opaque gelatinous

desert made with flavored corn starch and milk. In other words, one does not travel on a "golf junket," one takes a "golf tour."

Kick and spit

I have heard short par-four holes referred to obscenely as kick and spits. The British revere good short par fours, though. There is a great case for the occasional short par-four on every golf course. Tom Weiskopf, one of the greatest modern-day golf course designers, is also of that belief. Do not turn up your nose at holes of less than 350 yards because they can provide delightful challenges. Kick and spits, indeed!

Kick-in

A terrific approach shot or chip can leave the ball so close to the hole that it is called a kick-in.

Kingdom of spirits

The Emerald Isle of Ireland, where superstitions, sprites and leprechauns abound, as does Guinness, Harp, Murphy's and Jamieson's Irish Whiskey.

Knee-trembler

Sometimes called a "knee-knocker," and meant to refer to a putt of such tantalizing length that it causes the knees to knock with fear. In Britain, however, a "knee-trembler" is a dalliance while standing and bracing against a wall.

Knickers

Never use the word knickers to describe a male's trousers or slacks. The British definition of knickers is usually bloomers, which are the undergarments on a very large woman. If someone is said to have their "knickers twisted," it means that they are all excited about something.

Laconic
A compact swing can be laconic, and a quick match or handy beating can be a laconic affair.

Ladies' tees
There has been recent debate, spurred by the political correctness crowd, about whether ladies' tees should be referred to as "up tees." Since there are so many sets of tees now available for players of all skill and strength, I believe "ladies' tee" is wholly appropriate.

Lady of Rank
The most respected of TOUR wives indeed deserve such a title. The late Mrs. Arnold Palmer (Winnie) and the late Mrs. Ben Hogan (Valerie) were instrumental in their husband's successes. Mrs. Jack Nicklaus (Barbara), Mrs. Gary Player (Vivienne), Mrs. Bob Charles (Verity), are also held in very high esteem. Many wives of the modern-day TOUR pros are active in the PGA TOUR Wives Association, which organizes and promotes charitable events.

Land of fruits and nuts
California, home of the PGA TOUR's West Coast swing, which can also appropriately be called the "left coast swing." Gary McCord is from California.

Land of letters and poets
Ireland.

Lawn

A very nice green may sometimes be referred to as a lawn. Try not to use the nickname "dance floor" because everyone else does. During a CBS broadcast, I once commented on a poor shot into the green by saying, "He is on the dance floor...but the music will be faint!"

Laxity in holing out

Another bright euphemism meaning that you did not, by the strictest of rules, finish out your putts. Ken Venturi and other players afflicted with the yips are known for their laxity in holing out. However, this friendly gesture is perfectly acceptable in gentlemanly country club games.

If you and your fellow competitors are indeed conceding putts, do so graciously and without ceremony. Simply tell your opponent, "It's good" without delay or deliberation.

The most polite manner in which to concede a putt was displayed by Jack Nicklaus when he conceded the all-important two-foot putt to Tony Jacklin that resulted in Britain and Ireland's halving of the 1969 Ryder Cup matches at Royal Birkdale. Despite the incredible drama and significance of the moment, Nicklaus simply picked up Jacklin's marker and shook his hand. It was one of the most significant and dignified displays of sportsmanship in golf history.

Lay back

A lay back shot is designed to have the ball cease rolling at a distance from which it can be comfortably hit into the green. For instance, if a player cannot realistically reach the green, but knows that he can hit his best approach shot with a pitching wedge from 110 yards, he might run the ball down the fairway to that distance as opposed to just advancing it as far as he can. While it might seem to be a timid approach, the lay back is a good example of course management and strategy.

Lay up

A lay up shot is designed to avoid actually reaching its target, but rather, stopping as near to the danger that fronts it as possible. If a burn runs in front of the green, for instance, a player might choose to not attempt to carry the creek and hit a lay up shot safely short of it instead. This conservative strategy is intended to have the ball roll as close to the hazard as possible without challenging it.

The lay up shot is sometimes employed by competitors in the Masters Tournament on Augusta National's 15th hole. If the player's drive on the par-five is wayward, and he does not have a safe line to the green from an acceptable distance, he might hit a lay up to keep his ball from landing in the pond in front. This strategy takes eagle out of play, but also takes bogey out of play, and leaves birdie and par as the most likely results.

Leather mashie

When a scurrilous player uses his foot to covertly kick his ball in an attempt to improve his lie, he is said to have employed the use of the "leather mashie." The reference is to his shoe leather striking the ball as if it were an acceptable golf club. Why we afford cheaters such a light-hearted metaphor is beyond me, but in the interest of avoiding fisticuffs, sometimes only a euphemism will do.

Level par

Should be verbally employed rather than the phrase "even par."

As late as 1950, the standard for scoring was "level fours," which is to say that every score was assessed against an average of four on each hole. Eighteen fours equaled par 72. For instance, three 3's and 15 4's gave a player a score of "three under 4's." Eventually, score was measured against par, and players were said to be "under par," "over par," or level par.

Light housekeeping

A short putt that simply needs to be tapped-in or a match that is easily won.

Light of battle

There is no mistaking seeing the light of battle in someone's eyes. It is as if you can see the very reflection of the fire and flames! A player is likely to have the light of battle in his eyes when he is preparing for a match or about to head onto the golf course. It is the anticipation, the excitement and the stimulation inspired by competition.

Raymond Floyd used to get that look more than any player I have witnessed. In American football, it is sometimes called "putting your game face on," and Floyd had an intense game face like no other.

Lighting the cigar

The achievement of victory, or the late certain knowledge that victory is at hand. One can almost read on a player's face that he realizes victory is at hand. It is a flush feeling of relief and satisfaction, much like the draw of a fine victory cigar.

Limey

This term, commonly applied to British subjects, is actually a slur. British convicts that were deported to America via ships were fed limes to ward off potential scurvy. The insulting derivation was born of that indignation.

Lingering at the gates

Hanging around a lead but never quite getting out in front in the tournament.

Links

In America, the word has become slang for any golf course. A true links golf course, though, is only one that is built on the area of ground between the beach and the farming land that is covered with topsoil. This largely useless strip of land connects or "links" the beach with the fertile farming land. The reason many golf courses are built on linksland is that it features undulating ground and coarse grass growing on a sandy base. This rolling ribbon of treeless land near the seashore is good for little else other than a golf course, for which, it is eminently suitable.

Loathe to yield further amusement

A player who is trying to stop the bleeding and put the wheels back on during his round. Losing is embarrassing, and doing it in front of a gallery or against a rival, only adds insult to injury.

Longings of vengeance

The burning desire of a player to right a wrong that occurred on the golf course. An extreme example might be the angst that Ken Venturi felt when he lost the 1960 Masters Tournament to Arnold Palmer. Many felt that the tournament was going to be won by Venturi, but the green jacket evaded his grasp when a difficult ruling was made in Palmer's favor.

Loose impediments
Are natural objects not fixed or growing. Stones, leaves, and dung are examples of loose impediments.

Lunch ball
The often less than spectacular first tee shot on the first hole of play, perhaps due to the lunch preceding, is sometimes followed by a generously offered "lunch ball." This is another way to refer to a mulligan shot. For early tee times, the term "breakfast ball" might be more appropriate.

Majestic survey

The taking-in of the glorious view of a golf course with one's eyes before play. The course need not be dazzling or even scenic. But to the eyes of a real golfer, any patch on which the game is played is a majestic prospect.

Make the turn

Moving from the outward half to the inward half by going from the ninth green to the tenth hole. In the old days of "out and back" links golf courses, making the turn meant literally turning around and playing the second half of the golf course, which were holes that led back to the clubhouse.

Man and boy

When you have known someone for a great deal of their life, you might say that you have known them as man and boy. You needn't literally have known them since childhood to execute this phrase. Since we are all constantly aging, and some of us make the transition from boy to man at quite different ages, it is truly a colorful figure of speech!

Marked character

Bobby Jones, Jack Nicklaus, Tiger Woods, or other dominant players at the start of a tournament. Most would agree that it is one or more of these talented players versus the rest of the field.

Marker pole

Is a direction post to reveal the aiming point on holes that present blind shots. In some cases, rolling landscape and hills keep the green or fairway hidden from view. At Lahinch GC, the "St. Andrews of Ireland," a white painted rock is used to provide direction on the famous "Dell Hole," a par-three on which the entire green is hidden between two giant mounds.

Match play
The British and Irish most often play the game as it was intended to be played, which is to say, in match play format. In match play, each hole is worth one point, and the player with the lower score on a given hole is said to have "won the hole."

When a player has taken a six-hole lead and there are only five holes remaining, he is said to have beaten his opponent by "six and five." If he should take a three-hole lead with only two holes remaining, he has won by "three and two."

If the match goes to the final hole "all square" (meaning tied), and an outcome is determined there, the winner is said to have won "one-up." If a player clings to a one hole lead on the 18th tee, and then beats his opponent on that last hole, he is said to have won "two-up."

Measureless distance of conjecture
A blind shot to a hidden green or obscured fairway.

Member's bounce
A helpful and fortuitous stroke of providence that kicks a ball from the dark of the woods back into the light of the fairway is said to be a "member's bounce." The phrase facetiously presumes that the player, a member of the given club, receives lucky benefits as part of his club privileges.

Mercenary dependency
A professional golfer who will play in any silly season event or pro-am in an effort to fatten his wallet. Some TOUR players enter events simply in search of cash, never thinking about winning or the spirit of the game. Endorsement deals also brings out the mercenary dependency in some players.

Mixed gruesome
A chauvinist facetious term sarcastically used to refer to a "mixed foursome" in which men play along with women, which is still frowned upon at some of the more archaic golf clubs of the United Kingdom.

Mixed foursome
Is a match that is comprised of one man and one woman on each two-person team.

Mooning about
Slowly poking your way around a golf course, and perhaps visiting areas of it not previously tread upon by man or beast. Your frustrated companions might yell to you: "Quit mooning about and let's go!"

Moor
A tract of open, uncultivated upland, especially when covered with heather.

Mother and father of a hammering
A more than decisive victory over one's opponents. May also be used to describe a very violent, heavy thunderstorm that

interrupts a golf game.

Muirfield

When referring to the site of Jack Nicklaus' Memorial Tournament in Ohio, the name of the venue is Muirfield Village GC. Simply saying "Muirfield" is to refer to the original, exclusive Muirfield Club in Scotland. Don't confuse things.

Similarly, Troon GC is in Arizona. The original Troon— Royal Troon—is in Scotland.

Mulligan

A re-take or second chance at a missed shot. My advice, if your playfellows choose to insist on collecting mulligans, is that you demand that they forfeit their original shot once they've hit their mulligan ball. Once the mulligan ball is struck, they are left without the option of choosing either ball. I believe players would then more carefully consider whether they really want that mulligan.

Mulligans have no place in golf other than on the first tee.

Multiplicity of tasks

A putt with more than one break in it and of considerable uphill or downhill speed can leave a player feeling that he is faced with a multiplicity of tasks.

Muses of victory

Players at the highest level will often become dependant upon the services of sports psychologists or swing gurus for the motivation, mindset, or swing tips to urge them toward victory. Whether these psychologists or swing doctors are as valid as the imaginary muses of folklore has really never been determined, but the marketing machines behind them will insist so.

Nap

Is the British word for the grain of a putting surface, which is to say the direction in which the grass blades grow. The nap of a green can have a great deal of effect on the speed and break of putts. In South Africa, for instance, the grass is very wiry, creating nap of such formidable proportion that putts can actually break uphill! In other words, mind the nap.

Naturally tenacious

Gritty competitors like Steve Pate, Tommy Armour, Tommy Bolt, and Lee Trevino earn this distinction from me because they are emotional in their thirst for winning, a thirst that is unquenched until they are victorious.

Necessary ligature

In order for a Ryder Cup team to be successful, or for any foursomes or fourball team to play well together, there must be a necessary ligature or a bonding between the team members, players or partners.

Necessity of instruction

Players who cannot function without their swing guru or coach —such as Nick Faldo—suffer when performing alone. If you'd like to find a pleasant way to characterize the skills of a beginner after enduring a round in which he or she was unable to create anything even reminiscent of a golf shot, this description may also be employed.

Nerves of agitation

When a player is spooked by the gamesmanship of another,

he is battling nerves of agitation. Lee Trevino, Seve Ballesteros, Dave Hill and Tommy Bolt were known to inspire nerves of agitation.

Never up, never in

As the actress said to the Bishop. Never up, never in is actually a British expression, as is the risque reference to the two concerned. It means simply that if you don't putt your ball with enough speed to make it to the hole, it never has a chance to go in. Leaving putts short is really one of the worst crimes in golf, and nothing more that a very frivolous waste of opportunity.

The esteemed golf writer Bernard Darwin may have uttered this sentiment in a more picturesque manner by saying, "Fortune favors the brave at golf, and there never was yet a timid player who went by the nickname 'lucky.'"

Nipped and blanched

By the time of the final round, the greens at the United States Open are nipped and blanched.

No blood

A phrase to recap and characterize a halved hole in match play, inferring that no point was won, and therefore, no blood was spilled.

No bloody fear

Is a British phrase of emphatic agreement. It is akin to the American expressions: "Amen, brother!" "No doubt!" or "I hear that!"

Noble summits

A term reserved for those locations only immediately recognizable as the finest and most revered of clubhouses. The Royal and Ancient clubhouse at St. Andrews, the gleaming white, antique, antebellum structure at the Augusta National Golf Club, or the sprawling and suitable manse at Shinnecock Hills immediately come to mind.

Nursery of chosen plants

The Augusta National Golf Club, because it is built on the site of a former nursery. The nursery was once called "Fruitlands."

Nursling of the course

A player, like Davis Love III, who was raised around the game of golf and grew up on a golf course. Love, Arnold Palmer, and others grew up as the sons of golf professionals.

Oak tree legs

The first time I saw Jack Nicklaus in shorts, it was an eye-opener. He was in tennis garb at his home in Palm Beach, and it seemed as though he had Oak tree trunks for legs. I then realized that those trunk-like legs were a source for generating the enormous power in his golf swing.

Obeying the monitor

CBS producer Frank Chirkinian insisted that the air talent pay attention to what was on the television monitor while watching play on the golf course, a tactic that was sure to ensure a good broadcast.

Obviate the necessity

To avoid a playoff.

Odor of success

Can be sensed not only by one's rich apparel, cushy travel arrangements, media demands, but also by the manner in which a player carries himself.

Offensive weakness

A glaringly insufficient portion of a player's golf game. Putting, short game, or length off the tee could be an offensive weakness—offensive to the player or his partner!

Old Nick

British nickname for Satan.

On a jolly

Just out for fun. Many players travel to golf resorts "on a jolly."

On the pencil

When you are at a club or resort and you need only to sign all of your expenses and incidentals to a number because your charges are covered, you are said to be "on the pencil."

One-upsmanship

Is when a player attempts to steal the advantage back from his fellow competitor or opponent. It is the art of maintaining a psychological advantage by impressing and thereby distressing your opponent.

For instance, during the final round of the 1975 Masters, Jack Nicklaus, standing on the 16th green, was forced to watch Tom Weiskopf, directly across the pond on the 15th green, sink a ten-foot birdie putt to claim a one-shot lead. Under the watchful eye of the new leader, Nicklaus then calmly displayed perhaps the most bold example of one-upsmanship by sinking his 40-foot birdie putt to reclaim a share of the lead!

Of course, Nicklaus himself was a victim of one-upsmanship on the first tee of an 18-hole playoff for the 1971 United States Open Championship at Merion Country Club. Trevino, who lived on gamesmanship and one-upmanship, unnerved the stoic Nicklaus by tossing a rubber snake at him as they waited to hit their tee shots. Trevino went on to win the playoff.

Open graves of torture

Gaping and dangerous bunkers, such as Oakmont Country Club's "Church Pews" or the "Hell Bunker" on the Old

Course at St. Andrews.

Ordinary housekeeper

A PGA TOUR player that makes his living playing on the TOUR simply by sweeping-up bits of money each week but never contending for a victory.

Outside agency

Something which affects the ball or its position but is not a recognized or integral part of the game or golf course. An example of an outside agency could be an automobile, a sheep, or a train—all of which one of my golf balls has struck at one time of another. If a player's ball is carried off in the automobile, sticks in the animal, or is pushed down the train tracks by a locomotive, consideration is made within the rules.

I witnessed an occasion at the Players Championship where an osprey swooped down and plucked a player's ball from the surface of the famed island green at the 17th hole. The winged creature then lifted the ball to the skies, and dropped it into the pond. (In this situation, Rule 18-1 applies and no penalty is incurred. Because the ball was not immediately retrievable, the player was allowed to substitute a new ball.

While I was playing in the English Amateur Championship at Sunningdale, a workman, who qualified as an outside agency, plucked my ball from the rough and skipped it into his pocket. To my good fortune, my opponent witnessed and attested to the thievery.

Over the moon

Very excited, thrilled. A golfer can be just "over the moon" about a good shot or victory.

Overcooked

A delicious term to describe a putt or shot that has been hit too firmly. "Undercooked," on the other hand, describes a putt or shot that was not hit firmly enough to reach its intended destination.

Pains of the ascent

The unmentionable sacrifices that come with being a star player on the PGA TOUR. Demands for time, multiple interviews, large crowds, autograph requests, and the examination of one's private life all fit into this category. Example: Tiger Woods.

Painted holes

Televised PGA TOUR events, the inside of a golf hole is painted bright white to aid viewers in spotting it on the green. Another phrase, "painted it," is often used to describe a putt that grazes a cup without going in.

Paroxysm of emotions

The feelings, fears and palpitations that can affect a player near the end of a tournament. Greg Norman's misguided four-iron shot that missed the 18th green on the final hole of the 1986 Masters may have been caused by or provoked a paroxysm of emotions. Certainly, Doug Sanders felt them during the 1970 Open Championship, as did Jesper Parnevik during his closing hole at Turnberry in 1994.

Partners

Do not carelessly use the term partners to refer to the people that you are playing a round in the company of. In a three-ball or a two-ball competition, the others in your group should only be referred to as your partner if you are indeed teamed with them. I have heard the term "playing partner" used, but "playing" is unnecessary, and "partner" will do just fine. At CBS TV, we were instructed by producer/director Frank Chirkinian to refer to the other players on the golf course as "fellow competitors," a genteel term that I believe originated at The Masters.

Paucity of vocabulary

Is a synonym for many current American sports announcers. Paucity means a shortage, and the fact that you are reading this book is a meager step in the right direction for the future of literature and the Queen's English in golf.

One might also have paucity of length in his or her tee shots.

Paving hell with energy

Coming back from behind the field or somehow finding a way to rescue a bad round through never-say-die effort.

P.B.F.U

Stands for Post-birdie "foul"-up. PBFU is the maddening phenomenon experienced when a great birdie seems washed-away by a foolish miscue on the following hole.

Peculiarities of temper

The unpredictable manner in which temper can have an effect on a player's golf game. Rage, for some players, is a motivator. For others, tension and anger simply destroy the swing. Craig Stadler seems to always play angry. Lee Trevino had his moments of great temper. Tommy Bolt was a club thrower.

Pedestal of infamy

When a player is repeatedly reminded of a traumatic failure, they seem to be placed on a pedestal of infamy by the media and sometimes the galleries. Greg Norman's collapse at the

1996 Masters Tournament placed him on such a pedestal. When the loveable Roberto De Vicenzo mistakenly signed an incorrect scorecard, costing him a chance to compete in an 18-hole playoff at the 1968 Masters Tournament, he was forever placed on that pedestal.

Fairly or not, the conservative play that cost Chip Beck a chance to win at the Augusta National Golf Club in 1993 has also given him a lofty perch in infamy.

Peevish displeasure
A crusty and ill-natured manner of complaining about a bad shot or round.

Pellet
On occasion, I refer to the golf ball as a pellet. A pellet is a small ball of lead that is similar to the balls of lead (bullets) carried by the British forces during your Revolutionary War.

Perfectly judicious
When a player experiences a good bounce after getting a bad break on the previous hole, the situation is then perfectly judicious.

Perfidious hint
Sly swing tips or sneaky suggestions given to an opponent to disturb their routine or throw off their game.

Pestilent nook
A tough spot on the golf course from which to play. A steep bunker, dense forest, dangerous water hazard, or tricky

hillock might be a pestilent nook of the course.

PGA
Stands for Professional Golfers Association, but causes a great deal of confusion among the populace since a number of different organizations use the letters P-G-A in their names. Please allow me to help clear up some of the misconceptions:

The PGA TOUR
Is the organization of touring, tournament professionals who compete in golf events to earn their living. The PGA TOUR is comprised of "professional golfers." The PGA TOUR is headquartered in Ponte Vedra Beach, Florida. The PGA TOUR is a non-profit organization that stages tournaments to provide prize money for its players and raise money for local charities. Many of the PGA TOUR players are members of the PGA of America, which is an altogether different organization. The Tournament Players Division of the PGA of America split away from that organization in 1968 and later became known as the PGA TOUR.

The PGA of America
Is the organization of "golf professionals" who earn their living as head professionals and assistant professionals at golf clubs and golf courses, where they teach the game and promote golf through the sales of equipment and the organization of tournaments. The PGA of America is headquartered in Palm Beach Gardens, Florida. Each summer, the PGA of America stages the

PGA Championship, which is the Championship of the PGA of America, not the PGA TOUR. The PGA Championship is considered a major championship. PGA TOUR players and club professionals compete in this event.

Phlegmatic

During the final round of his 1993 Masters Tournament victory, I described Bernhard Langer as "the imperturbable, phlegmatic one." This meant that Langer was impassive, deliberate, calm, and utterly oblivious to the pressure. He simply went about his business...and won.

Pilgrim's staff

When a player strolls along carrying a golf club like a walking stick, the club might be referred to as a pilgrim's staff. (See cudgel.)

Plainly destined for stardom

I once (incorrectly) described Japanese professional golfer Tommy Nakajima with this phrase. If your partner gets off to a good start during one of your rounds, you might bolster him with this phrase of hyperbole. However, it might also destroy his round.

Play through

See "give way."

Plumb bob

I'm afraid I look askance at players who insist on plumb-bobbing, which is the act of dangling the putter vertically over the line of a putt and peering at the shaft in an effort to determine the break. When playing with an amateur who insists on going through the time-consuming ritual of plumb bobbing on every hole, I always insist on asking them what they are doing. Very few can even answer the question, but since they see it on television, they choose to mimic the TOUR pros.

Plus fours
The baggy, short pants that the older gentlemen wear. Plus twos and plus fours serve as very practical attire for golf since their shortness prevents mud from collecting on what otherwise would be longer trousers.

Plus twos
The proper way to refer to the quite tight fitting, Payne Stewart-type garb, which are the short pants that end at the knees and are often incorrectly called "knickers."

Pommie
The Australian term for a British person. It's an ironic and insulting name meaning "Prisoner of her Majesty." It's taken from "POHM" which was stenciled on the uniforms of the British prisoners who were shipped off to Australia. There's no love lost between Britain and Australia. The Australians call the Brits "Whinging Poms," and we call them "Dirty Diggers."

Pompous level of childhood
The cockiness of youth.

Pourboire

From the French we gather this dashing manner of referring to a gratuity or tip that you might give a locker room attendant, club valet, caddie, and most appropriately a bartender. Pourboire is pronounced (poor-bwaar.)

Pouring scorn

To lay blame or verbally criticize your partner or opponent. While others are "chewing someone out," you should "pour scorn." You might pour scorn on a cheater or a partner who is not playing up to his ability.

Power of no good

Hitting lengthy but wayward drives.

Prattle of children

When spoiled PGA TOUR players gripe or complain about their amenities. They collect the keys to courtesy cars, devour free meals, and practice and play on courses of only the finest conditions for the biggest of purses. There is nothing, really, that the American TOUR player could ever have to complain about.

Precipice

Similar yet more severe than an escarpment, a precipice defines the perilous ridge. It is a most vertical and steep face of a cliff. Because of its severity, one is either on the edge of a precipice or they are hastening to their death below. The descent from a precipice is precipitous. The cliff top along the eighth hole at Pebble Beach is a precipice. In fact, two Japanese businessmen playing golf at Pebble Beach were deep in conversation and quite accidentally drove an automotive golf cart over the side of that precipice and fell to their doom.

Pre-round Advil
The quick swallow is advised before a golf game to soothe the muscles of those over the age of 50.

Preternatural length
Players who hit the ball as far as Tiger Woods and John Daly are players of preternatural length.

Prisoner in his own backyard
The host of one's own tournament might be considered a backyard prisoner since it is most difficult and even unlikely that he could ever win his tournament on his home course. The demands of hosting, organizing and representing the event are simply too cumbersome.

Arnold Palmer has felt the responsibility of being the host at his Bay Hill Invitational, Jack Nicklaus is the figurehead of his Memorial Tournament at Muirfield Village (which, of course, he did win once), and even Tiger Woods struggled in the inaugural Williams World Challenge event he hosted at Grayhawk in Arizona. Doug Sanders once hosted a Senior TOUR event in Texas, and Greg Norman hosts his yearly Shark Shootout (which has recently moved from California to Miami).

Professional's shop
Is the very British way to refer to what many inappropriately call a "Pro Shop." Commonly, the area in which one goes to

settle their green fees or make ancillary purchases of golf accessories is the Professional's Shop," which is managed by the resident Golf Professional.

Profound stillness of silence
The dead calm moment before an important shot or putt. Despite throngs of gathered gallery, a whisper is enough to break this chilling and anticipatory moment. It can also be referred to as a "deafening silence."

Profusion of color
Aptly describes the wardrobe of colorful Texan Doug Sanders, who may have owned more pairs of shoes than Imelda Marcos.

Put them to flight
Is a good way to say that you've beaten up on your opponents, and have defeated them handily. "We put those buggers to flight, didn't we?"

Quartet

Is four players having a go 'round the golf course. Saying that you "have a foursome" is a wretched misuse of the word. A genuine "foursome" translated means four players, partnered in twos, each team playing only one ball in an alternate shot fashion. A "four-ball" is when each player plays with his own ball, and those players play in a "quartet." In a quartet, one plays his individual instrument, just as a player in a golf quartet plays his or her own ball. You may play foursomes in a quartet, or you can have a four-ball with a quartet. Simple, right?

Rabbit, run!

Is a stylish phrase you might shout in an effort to audibly implore your ball to roll further. It likely will have no effect on the ball, you understand, but it will serve the dual role of helping you to release your anguish and impressing your fellow competitors by giving tribute to American literary giant John Updike, who titled his most famous work with the same phrase.

Rats

European Tour players and golfers in England have sometimes referred to their caddies as "rats." In earlier days, caddies were a rough and rugged bunch, unshaven, and wearing tattered clothing. In their ale-swilling, meager existence, some of them slept in bunkers, and at the approach of winter, would purposefully commit a crime to insure that they would be jailed and fed through the colder months. Choosing the proper crime was an art, since the rats wanted to be released in spring to caddie once again.

I don't advise you calling your caddie a rat. Take the time to learn his name instead. It will make for a much nicer round.

Ratting cap

The traditional style of cap worn by Ben Hogan, Byron Nelson, Ken Venturi, and in the modern game, was worn by Payne Stewart. The body of the flat cap is buttoned or stitched or connected by studs to the bill.

Before popular use in golf, these stitch-down caps were worn by the fellows who were employed to catch rats on the streets of London.

Rave of furious gusts and torrents

The biggest of rain and windstorms common to Scotland and Great Britain.

Ready golf

Means hit it when you get to it, and let's get our round finished before Boxing Day!

Rebellion against par

When par is under assault in a tournament, usually due to an easy course and windless weather conditions. After a rain, when greens hold very well, players can stage a rebellion against par. Sometimes, as in the cases of Al Geiberger, Chip Beck, and David Duval, a single player can do it in a single round. All three have shot the PGA TOUR single-round record of 59.

Regaining your equilibrium

When a player suffers through a slump of unmentionable scores during a round and then recovers with a birdie or par, he's surely regained his equilibrium!

Registering wrongs

Writing down a poor result on a scorecard.

Release

In many cases when a player hits a pitch and run or run up shot, he will see the ball land short and verbally beg it to "release!" If the ball is rolling too hot for the hole, he will ask instead to "bite."

While they may sound like terms of intended technique, I assure you that they are merely cries of desperate anguish!

Relinquishing all interference

Closing out the world in an effort to focus on one's game. When a player walks through a gallery from green to tee and doesn't even acknowledge that anyone else is on the course with him, he has relinquished all interference. This type of player might also be oblivious to gamesmanship and might also ignore the advice of his caddie or coach.

Remarkable knack of narrative

British golf writer and television announcer Henry Longhurst, who was my mentor, had an incredibly compelling manner of telling a story, and so therefore had a remarkable knack of narrative. My longtime friend and colleague Jack Whitaker, who presented brilliant on-air essays, also possessed this enjoyable and unique talent.

Remote and mysterious regions

When a ball is hit to areas of the golf course not previously visited by golfers, and with which even the caddies are wholly unfamiliar.

Replete catalog of accomplishments

The greatest of Champions carry the full catalog of accomplishments. Only Gene Sarazen, Ben Hogan, Jack Nicklaus and Gary Player have won all four of the modern major championships.

Reposing in the autumn

Putting the clubs away until the next spring.

Respectable poverty

Players who slug it out to earn a living on mini-tours and circuits like the Buy.Com Tour and the Hooters Tour.

Resuming the empire

When a successful player wins another major championship, especially after sometime without. There can be no denying that when Jack Nicklaus won the 1980 United States Open, he savored the victory. It had been five years since that thoroughbred had been trotted to the winner's circle. (Later that same year, he also won the PGA Championship.)

Right in the lumberyard

In the golf film "Caddyshack," Chevy Chase's character Ty Webb attempts to bolster the confidence of Bushwood Country Club caddie Danny Noonan. Noonan, who had college aspirations, was worried that he might not be talented enough for higher education, and feared spending his life working in a lumberyard. Webb tries to get Noonan in touch with his "zen" by having him hit golf balls while blindfolded. Noonan, unable to see, hits his first ball into the water, and asks Webb where it went. "Right in the lumberyard," Webb deadpanned.

Use that line on one of your fellow competitors sometime.

Royal

This designation—as in Royal Melbourne Golf Club, Royal Montreal Golf Club, Royal Aberdeen Golf Club, and Royal

West Norfolk Golf Club—can only be bestowed by a reigning monarch. Typically, the monarch has indeed played the golf course before bestowing the designation. Royal is a rare designation when one considers that there have not been very many golfers among the recent reigning monarchs.

Edward VIII, who later became the Duke of Windsor, was the last reigning monarch that was keen on the game. It is rumored that Edward the VIII took away the Royal designation from Berkshire Golf Club because they would not allow his friend Archie Compston into their clubhouse.

The world's only nine-hole golf course with the Royal designation is Royal Worlington and Newmarket.

St. Andrews

Is a town, not a golf course. The birthplace of golf is called "The Old Course," and to be even more correct one usually says "The Old Course at St. Andrews."

There are plenty of other golf courses in St. Andrews, by the way. The New Course, Jubilee, Eden and the Dukes course are just a few.

Saddle

If the fairway slopes up on either side with mounds, and your ball is in between, you are in the saddle of the hole.

Sand scrape

You may refer to a shallow bunker as a "sand scrape." American courses, especially in Florida, feature sand scrapes, which are very shallow bunkers that are not very penal in nature.

Sandbagger

To 'sandbag' is literally to barricade, defend, or coerce by harsh means. I never knew the word's meaning in golf until I came to America. In my opinion it's a generous euphemism for one who plainly cheats on his handicap in order to protect his chances of winning and coerce victory from his opponent.

I played in the Heritage Classic Pro-Am one year with Dave Stockton. Also in our group was a corporate CEO who purported to have a USGA Handicap Index of 17. We won the tournament, but it was a joyless victory because immediately following the awards presentation, Stockton followed the man into the parking lot, grabbed him by his shirt, and went nose to nose with him.

"I want you to know that I got no satisfaction from that so-called 'win,'" Stockton growled at the CEO. "You're a sandbagger and I hope I never see you again, let-alone play golf with you."

This "17-handicap" had shot a 74.

Sands of time have run out

This was the way I described Tom Watson's unsuccessful attempt to catch-up with Seve Ballesteros in the 1983 Masters Tournament.

Scatterings of ability

Good shots every now and again, scattered through a golf round like apple seeds over an orchard.

Scorecard playoff

When the need to play extra holes to determine a winner is not available for one reason or another—and a tournament must end with an outright winner—matching scores from the scorecard is often the way this determination is made. Some times this is done by starting with the 18th hole and going backwards, and some times it's done by beginning with the number-one handicap hole and working down.

Scratch golfer

Is an amateur who is expected to shoot close to par more often than not. "Expert" is another way to refer to this player and his admirable skills.

Scurrilously

Because of Seve Ballesteros' many mishaps at the Augusta National Golf Club's 15th hole, I once surmised that that hole had dealt scurrilously with him. To be treated scurrilously is to be shown insolence, disrespect, and even—in the case of the talented Ballesteros — blasphemy.

Searching eyes

The manner in which a player's eyes shift and scan the skies searching for the ball flight and trying to estimate where exactly it will land while keeping track of its position.

Secretary

In Britain, a club secretary is not a secretary in the vein of the American administrative assistant. A club secretary in Britain is the person who serves as the manager of, and the most important man or woman at, a golf club. A club secretary does not take dictation, but rather, dictates.

Seducer

Someone who attempts to sweet-talk a golf ball in flight in an effort to convince it to fly in the proper direction. It's usually in vain.

Selling sweep

Sometimes known as a "Calcutta," this is a wagering system in which players from a tournament field are auctioned-off and wagered on before a competition.

Sending it to perdition

Launching a golf ball into a pond or deep in the woods, or perhaps even over a cliff, to a place from whence it will never return.

Sequence of horrid imprecations

A string of curses or calamitous utterances by a player, usually following a shot found to be particularly disgusting. Craig Stadler, if watched closely, seems to verbalize a permanent sequence of horrid imprecations that equal his blustery stream of consciousness.

Sequestered plantation

The exclusive and guarded confines of the Augusta National Golf Club. (See "silent nursery")

Shank

A poorly miss hit and embarrassing shot that sends the ball bounding away sideways on nearly a 90-degree angle from the player's aim of address. You should avoid ever using this word for fear of invoking the appearance of the mysterious, uninvited shot.

Shave strokes

Is to erroneously record a number on the scorecard lower than the number genuinely scored. Stroke shavers never win in the long run, however, because, when reported, the deceitful scores will improperly lower the cheaters handicap to a level at which he cannot realistically compete.

Shellacking
A sound beating such that the loser feels as though they've been hunted, felled, and sent through a visit to the taxidermist. Made to feel antiquated.

Shocked the pupils
When a former champion makes a stunning run at a tournament title in the late years of his career, it always surprises (and some times scares) the younger players. Ben Hogan did this at the Cherry Hills U.S. Open in 1960 and again at the 1966 Masters. Jack Nicklaus shocked the pupils by winning the 1986 Masters, and then by making a strong run at the same tournament in 1998.

Shoppe
I refuse to frequent any establishment that refers to itself as a "shoppe" instead of a shop. The addition of an extra "p" and an extra "e" is a ridiculous and pompous affectation designed to add an air of quaint whimsy. Similarly, beware of any golf course with a superfluous "e" onto the end of the name. I suppose that golf course owners feel that with a name such as Boulder Pointe or Olde English GC, they can command an extra $15 in green fees.

Shoulders of whalebone and iron
A partner who must carry an inferior partner successfully must have attributes such as these.

Shrines of memory and immortality
The special spots on which golf history has been made and

commemorated. The Hogan and Sarazen bridges at the Augusta National Golf Club are such shrines. Augusta also has features to honor Palmer and Nicklaus, and there's a plaque at Royal Birkdale for Palmer and one at Hoylake for Bobby Jones.

Shrinking from arrogance
The act of an enlightened player who finally, through maturity, embraces a humble manner. Steve Pate, Raymond Floyd, the late Payne Stewart, and other once-cocky swells have undergone the transformation.

Silent nursery
The Augusta National Golf Club during the summer months between May and October when the club is closed. The Augusta National Golf Club was conceived and built by Bobby Jones with Alister Mackenzie on the site of a Georgia nursery.

Silent weapon
Perhaps no weapon in the arsenal of a golfers carries a more deadly value than a mind capable of great concentration and determination.

Silver jugs and crystal tankards
Tournament trophies.

Sin wasteful sins
To make silly mistakes during a round of golf. If one is to sin, by all means, make it a worthwhile sin. Missing a tap-in putt is to perpetrate a wasteful sin. Attempting to pull of a bold shot but missing is at least a worthy crime.

Singing of angels

As the song lyric claims, in the lilt of Irish laughter you can hear the angels sing. Of course, on the golf course, one might laugh when a shot off-line kicks off of a tree and is delivered back into the fairway. Surely one might hear the angels singing after helping a shot like that, and it likely is music to the players' ears.

Sinking under the wont of success

Trying too hard or pressing.

Smiling through cold teeth

Grinning and perhaps shaking the hand of an opponent one secretly despises. When you congratulate someone with false enthusiasm or be cordial in agreement without actually agreeing, you are said to be smiling through cold teeth.

Smoking gun

The "hot" putter of a player who has just sunk another of several important putts.

Sneaking wolfishly

Gaining on the pack in a quiet, aggressive manner, or closing in on an opponent in a match.

Sneaky long

During a CBS broadcast of The Masters Tournament, I once described Tom Kite as sneaky long. The lesson is that you mustn't always associate great length with the stature of a player. Size doesn't matter...in golf. Golfers like Kite, Gary

Player, Jeff Sluman and Corey Pavin are all slight of stature but sneaky long.

Snowman

I have never heard of an eight on the scorecard referred to as a snowman until I came to America, and I don't much like it. An eight already has enough ways to be referred to. It can be called an eight, a triple-bogey on a par-five, or a quadruple-bogey on a par-four. If you make an eight on a par-three, I'd recommend you not refer to it at all!

Sobbed-off his terror

A player who finds some way to handle his emotions and hold his game together through the penultimate and home holes. Some players whistle when facing a difficult shot, some breathe deeply, and though I've yet to see any sob, it wouldn't surprise me because there is now so much money at stake.

Sod revetment

Blocks of sand stacked to create what looks like a brick-faced bunker wall and lip.

Soft spikes

Even though this is a brand name, it is the simplest way to refer to the rubber spikes that have revolutionized the health and safety of bent grass greens everywhere.

Solitary churchyard

One of golf's hallowed venues standing quietly unoccupied in the rain. When heavy rains render a golf Mecca like Pebble

Beach, the Old Course at St. Andrews, or Augusta National unplayable, it is akin to a solitary churchyard.

Sorrows of Pope

"When sorrows come, they come not in single spies but in battalions." Alexander Pope's words might come to the mind of a player who slips into a slump during a round, and finds himself experiencing one bad break after another.

Sotto voce

Italian phrase meaning distant, "with a soft or quiet voice." Keep your conversations on the golf course sotto voce.

Sour grapes

Is an expression used to describe someone who is experiencing the taste of "sour grapes," which is to say that they are promoting resentful disparagement of something that they cannot personally acquire.

When the European Ryder Cup team lost the 1999 match, they began criticizing the sportsmanship of the Americans and took offense at the jubilation the yanks displayed in victory. I said then, and I maintain now, that the Europeans had a bloody load of sour grapes in their mouths and in their underwear, which is where I hope they shall stay.

Spike-guarded wall of defense

Gorse bushes that tightly line a fairway or any painful obstacle to success on a golf course.

Spinach
Another acceptable and colorful slang term to describe thick rough.

Splendid engraving
The joyful act of penciling a great number on the scorecard.

Starting time
One begins a round of golf by going to the tee at his appointed "starting time"—not at his "tee time." "Tea time" is half-past four every afternoon, though a true Brit drinks tea at anytime. Refer to your golf appointment as a starting time.

State of the mien
The attitude of greatness displayed by cocksure players like Jack Nicklaus, Tiger Woods, Ben Hogan, Ken Venturi, David Duval, and Tom Watson.

Stop the rot
The effort to make a good score on a hole, or even a single good shot in the hopes that you can rescue a round gone bad. A birdie after a streak of bogeys might, indeed, stop the rot. Winning a hole after going three-down might also stop the rotting or deterioration of your game and match.

Stymie
Is no longer a part of golf. In the old days, if Player A putted his ball and it stopped between his Player B's ball and the hole, Player B would have to somehow circumvent Player A's ball to get his own into the hole. Player A was not required

to mark and remove his ball.

If you were in the situation that Player B was in, you might try to impart sidespin on the ball to curve your putt around the stymie (Player A's ball), or putted to try to hit the edge of the hole. Sometimes a player was forced to simply play "safe away" (to the side). Some players also chipped or pitched their balls over the one in their way in an attempt to sink their shot.

If a player purposely positioned his ball such as to block his opponent from having a line to the hole, he was said to have "laid him a stymie." Indeed, championships were won and lost due to stymies.

In those earlier days, the stymie was generally accepted as being a part of the game. Over time, though, the practice came to be thought of as unfair and it was eventually abolished in the 1950s. When the stymie was still in use, however, playing a golf match was like contesting in a game of snooker or billiards. Personally, I thought the stymie was an evil practice.

Suffer no resurrection
When a player refuses to let up on an opponent, the opponent suffers no resurrection.

Summer rules
In England, the term summer rules is one that applies to the order and rule of drinking. When someone visits your home for an evening's fun in a casual setting, you might invoke summer rules. This informs your guests that you will pour the first drink for them, but after that, they are free and required to serve themselves and satisfy their thirst as they see fit.

Summoned for chastisement

This is when a player is called on the carpet and must appear at the office of PGA TOUR Commissioner to explain a transgression or display of poor sportsmanship. The late Clifford Roberts, in his role as Chairman of the Masters Tournament, frequently frightened invitees by occasionally demanding a meeting in his office. The reason they were so frightened was because they were afraid they had done something that would cause them not to be invited to The Masters again.

TOUR players Ken Green and John Daly have been summoned a few times in their careers.

Sunnier bloom

The happy look of a player who has pulled out of a slump or a streak of bad holes.

Superfluous lags the veteran on the stage

Golf writer Bernard Darwin used this phrase to describe a past-his-prime golfer who competes in a ceremonial fashion and cannot actually be a factor in a tournament or championship.

Should you be clinging to life in a match, fighting elimination but are obviously destined to be beaten, do everyone a favor and tap-in your putts and get out of the way. Superfluous lags the veteran on the stage.

Symphony of genius

The grateful applause of an assembled gallery in response to an excellent shot or excellent round.

Tam O'Shanter

Is a beret-type cap featuring a pom-pom on the top, and beloved item of clothing of the Scots. In many cases, the round woolen or cloth cap of Scottish origin is plaid. The Tam O'Shanter fits closely around the brow but is large and full above.

Tea and sympathy

Alas, while one rarely gets sympathy on the golf course, one can get a cup of tea. "Tea and Sympathy" is a pleasant enough English expression, but it becomes a sarcastic one when used on the golf course. Don't expect your fellow competitors or playing partners to give you sympathy when your game suffers. It is unbecoming.

Tee

A tee is a tee, and I do not condone the use of the slang nickname "Peg." Please use wooden tees on the golf course. Plastic tees are verboten. Of course, in the early days before manufactured tees, a player had to fashion a little pyramid of sand and rest his ball on it in preparation for every tee shot.

I try always like to play with white tees. I despise black tees because they make me feel as if I am in mourning for my departed game. A very pale, pink tee is too feminine. Natural wood- grain tees are also appropriate and tasteful.

Wade Hampton Golf Club in Cashiers, North Carolina allows only white tees and white golf balls to be used on its golf course. A mandate like that, however, may be going too far.

Tee box

The teeing ground on a golf course is sometimes frequently

referred to as the "tee box." This is because of the previously mentioned sand that was used in the old days to build a tee for a player's ball. Back then there was always a box full of sand near the teeing area. Today, there is often a container of sand or fertilizer near the teeing ground so that players can fill their divots after they've played a shot.

Tee it up

Golfers should not use the term "tee off." They either "start," "drive off," or hit their "tee shots" after "teeing it up." "Teed off," describes being angry with your opponent, or better yet "put off," or better yet "put upon." You might be teed off, put off, or put upon, but wait until after you have driven off with your tee shot to confront your opponent.

Tee markers

Objects that indicate the area of a teeing ground. Golf courses now present several locations from which to play on a given hole. In order to accommodate players of varying skill, experience, age and gender, you might encounter the following color code for tee markers: (This color-coding, from longest to shortest, is virtually standard at golf courses everywhere.)

NOTE: Tips

Some players insist on playing from the very back of the tee boxes in order to stretch the course to its maximum length, regardless of where the farthest tee markers are placed on a given day.

Black tees
The longest legitimate tee markers on a golf course, and therefore the sternest test available.

Blue tees
Also known as the "championship tees," and traditionally used for competition only. Advances in modern equipment, however, have driven the more-skilled players to the blue tees in search of a challenge. Unfortunately, too many high-handicap golfers are foolishly playing from these tees and are not only getting beat up, they're also slowing down golf courses.

White tees
Also known as the "member tees" and "men's tees," they are placed in the location that the golf course was designed to be played from most often. Players of even average skill should be able to manage the golf course from the white tees.

Gold tees and Silver tees
Are sometimes called the "senior tees." A course is shorter from these tees and more forgiving for the older players.

Red Tees
Are traditionally known as the ladies' tees, which though the shortest, can provide a great test of golf for the ladies if properly placed.

Green tees

Some golf courses have now taken to placing green tees in a position advantageous for beginners, learners, and juniors.

When playing as a guest at a golf club, it is always appropriate to play from the member tees. A proper guest does turn-up his nose at the member tees by insisting on flexing his muscles at the blue tees. Even worse are players who insist on playing any tees behind the white tees when their skill-level plainly doesn't match-up to the challenge.

Tempest of yelping

When TOUR players clamor for a lead in a tournament, all battling away in an effort to be heard from.

Temporary sojourner

When a player has a short-lived contact with the lead in a tournament, it makes this player a temporary sojourner. If he continues to play poorly, he might also be a temporary sojourner on the PGA TOUR.

Tentative prod

A putt made with uncertainty and with a stroke lacking enough confidence to firmly get the ball to the hole. A sure sign of a player who is nervous or feeling the pressure.

Terminating his command

Losing a lead or relinquishing an advantage in a tournament or match. A player might also be said to have terminated the command of his own game when he seems to lose control of his skill, usually due to pressure.

Texas wedge

Is an American slang word to describe a putter when used anywhere but on the green. Why Texans think they have a right to claim the origin of employing a putter from off of the green is beyond me, since the putter has been used from the aprons and fairways of the Old Course at St. Andrews, Scotland for over 500 years. Texas is, indeed, known for strong winds and firm golf courses on which the ball rolls a long way. Perhaps instead of Texas Wedge, however, a better term might be the "Bonnie Wedge."

The age of excuses

When the aches, pains and ailments begin to outnumber the pars, birdies and eagles.

The ascent to his garret

When a player climbs to the top of the leader board or the top of the money list, he's made an ascent to his position on top of the field.

The grip

The CBS broadcast team's nickname for PGA TOUR player Ed Fiori. The nickname refers to the extremely "strong" hands position that Fiori uses when swinging a golf club.

The last

Some television announcers, in an effort to affect a British air, have taken to referring to the 18th hole as "the last." I am not an advocate of this trend. The 18th hole should be called "the 18th hole."

The Open

The British Open may be referred to simply at "The Open" because it was the very first Open Championship. Having first been played in 1860, it predates all others. Some refer to the American Championship simply by saying "the Open," but you must—at minimum—say "U.S. Open" when referring to the United States Open Championship." I think simply saying U.S. Open is a little lazy.

The trail of Havana

Getting close to the leaders or attempting to pull away from the pack is to be on the trail of Havana. (See "Lighting the cigar.")

Theatrical reverence

Some of the PGA TOUR players really know how to charm the pants off of their pro-am partners, sponsors and hosts. Gary Player, for instance, when asked his opinion of a new golf course following a round, often answers the question by paying this theatrical reverence: "This is the finest golf course of its kind." At first glance, it sounds like high praise. But read it again. Does it really mean anything?

Three-ball

A three-ball match is supposed to give way to a foursomes (alternate shot) match on the golf course, but has equal standing to a four ball match in which each golfer is playing his own ball. This is a very good guideline and point of etiquette to promote speedy play on the golf course.

Threesome
Two players sharing one ball in an alternate-shot format against a single competitor playing his own ball.

Through the green
Is an expression that is meant to encompass all of the land that lies between tee and green on all 18 holes of a golf course. Every bit of land that is in play and in bounds is 'through the green.'

Throwing down rain
When heavy showers distract or interrupt a golf game, it is said to have been throwing down rain.

Tiger's contumacy
The absolute refusal of Woods to accept any boundaries in his quest for success and accomplishment. Each time he tees it up he's bent on winning—in spite of the field, the odds, the venue or the pressure.

Time immemorial
Forever remembered.

Too much pile
A slow green can be said to have too much pile, similar to a thick or shag carpet.

Tournament winner

A tournament is won by a tournament winner. He is not to be called a champion unless it was a championship tournament that he won. He is simply a tournament winner. In other words, there isn't a "champion" of the Bell South Classic, Buick Challenge or even The Masters Tournament.

Tourney

There isn't any such thing as a tourney. It is awful slang, and as such, to be totally disregarded. An organized game of golf should be referred to as a tournament, a competition, a match, or a championship.

Tradesman's entrance

Metaphorical term meaning the back of the hole. When the golf ball curls around hole and drops in the back, it has gone in through the tradesman's entrance. For instance, when the domestic staff, repairmen, plumber, painter or construction types enter a residence, they properly do so through the back door, or service entrance. Instead of using the formal front door, they gain access through the tradesman's entrance.

Tranquility of condemned doom

It is an awful feeling, but sometimes a player must play out the holes or complete a match after the cold realization that the drama of it has passed, and that an undesirable result is plainly evident. It is a release of tension, followed by a cloud of gloom.

Tranquility of inexpressible success

The calmness and aura that emanates from a winning player. When one observes Jack Nicklaus in almost any setting, he has a confidence and a tranquility that undeniably comes from the certain knowledge of his place in the game.

Transitory Power

A fluid and strong swing generates power through the body.

Trolley

A trolley is the mechanical device with a wheel support and a handle on which a golf bag may be placed and then pulled. A trolley is sometimes called a caddie car, which is preferable to the term "pull cart."

It has been said that the frequent pulling of a caddie car can lead to an ailment called "trolley-puller's bottom," which is a soreness in the upper buttocks. The antidote reportedly is to push the trolley from time to time instead of always pulling it over hill and dale.

Troubled spirit

It would be easy to attach this label to John Daly, who has suffered from bouts with alcohol, gambling, divorce and bankruptcy, but there have, in fact, been many troubled spirits on the PGA TOUR. At times, every golfer must have felt like a troubled spirit, since the game is so mentally demanding and sometimes torturous to the soul.

Turbulent impulse of nature

It can be difficult for a player to maintain his composure and keep his emotions in check due to the quite palpable turbulent impulse of nature.

'Twas Ever Thus

When the predictable outcome of a match occurs true to form, it 'twas ever thus. When a more skilled player defeats his inferior rival once again, it might say that the lesser player should have known better, since it 'twas ever thus. It is a resignation that circumstances are now no different than they ever have been—in golf, or in any aspect of life, really.

Twitches

Is the British equivalent of "yips." The twitches is a mysterious and largely psychological ailment that causes golfers to miss even the shortest of putts. Maddening and striking without reason or logical explanation, the twitches will provoke a severe loss of confidence in players who must suffer the sight of lipped, jabbed, pulled, and pushed putts.

Ungovernable excitement

The United States Ryder Cup teams' much-criticized jubilant celebration after Justin Leonard's putt to clinch a come-from-behind win at the 1999 match, was a good example of simple ungovernable excitement.

United Kingdom

When referring to Northern Ireland, Wales, Scotland or England, one may use the collective term The United Kingdom. The Republic of Ireland is technically no longer a part of Great Britain, and may be referred to simply as "Ireland."

Universal manifestation of discontent

When a group of players all begin to play poorly, as if bad golf was contagious, a universal manifestation of discontent has probably settled in.

Unjust severity

A bad bounce or an exceedingly unlucky break.

Vacant majesty

When a superstar player fails to be a factor in a tournament or plays far below his capabilities, he is said to be vacant majesty.

Vapid listlessness

A dull and colorless golf round is due to the vapid listlessness of the competitor.

Vexatious phlegm

The annoying indifference and sluggishness of an opponent or even a partner.

Voice of the Master

The delivery of an acceptance speech by a victorious and (hopefully) humble winner.

Volume of verse

A player who talks a great deal during the round.

W/C

The sight of these letters on the golf course might provide welcome relief to you. They signify "Water Closet," especially in the United Kingdom, where the facilities are also sometimes referred to as the "Loo." I much prefer water closet or loo to the less gracious terms of porta-john or rest room.

Wagering

Try to use the word wagering and not the rather more plebian term "betting."

There are countless ways to back your golf skills with a few shillings, and many ways to wager on the golf course. The method of using a "bisqe" is very sporting and traditional British manner of doing things.

Waggle

Letting a club swing freely at address in order to keep the wrists and joints loose during the swing and eliminate nervous tension.

Wand

An affectionate name for a hot putter. When a player is making all of his putts—from a variety of distances—it is, after all, pure magic.

Watery grave

Was an expression coined by the legendary British television announcer and golf writer Henry Longhurst, who used it to describe a golf ball that met an untimely "burial at sea."

Waxed lachrymose

A golfer who burdens his playfellows with sad and constant tales of his woes on the golf course is boring them by waxing lachrymose. (See "Tea and Sympathy.")

Wedge war

When two partners or fellow competitors are faced with short shots of equal length and challenge, one may audibly declare wedge war upon the other and place a wager upon which of the two will forge a better result with the shot.

Whilst

I do not subscribe to the British version of while. Though I see it in common use, I find it to be a sloppy deformation of the English language. In an English hotel, you might find a little sign in the loo that reads: "Please close curtain whilst showering." Follow the instructions regardless.

X

An "x" written where a number should be on a scorecard indicates that a player has surrendered to the golf course and the inferiority of his skills on a given hole. With no more desire for embarrassment or folly, the player has saved himself, and more importantly the rest of the players in his group, from the indignity of finishing out the hole in double digits. In other words, he has picked up his ball. X marks the spot in keeping up the pace and avoiding slow play.

X-Out

An imperfect golf ball that is sold by manufacturers at a discount price. The claim is that the only imperfection is a printing smudge or mistaken label. And if true, using x-outs might seem like an economically sensible tactic, were it not for the stigma that goes with being seen teeing-up one or plucking one from the hole.

Yes, sir!

Was an expression I blurted out during the CBS broadcast of the 1986 Masters Tournament. Jack Nicklaus, on his way to a popular win and a sixth green jacket, lined up his attempt to sink what would be a pivotal putt for an eagle-three at the par-five 15th hole. As Jack's ball crept over the edge of the cup and disappeared into the hole, I shouted "Yes, sir!"

Yips

See "Twitches."

Zealousness

Eagerness or youthful enthusiasm for competition. While a younger, less established player competes week after week with unbridled zealousness, an older, more successful player paces himself, carefully choosing which tournaments to play in and when to take time off of the TOUR. Zealousness can also lead to first-found jitters or too much emphasis on the beginning of a tournament.

Zenith

The top of one's playing career, when he's reached the finest form he's ever likely to enjoy. Despite all of his earlier wins, Mark O'Meara's 1998 season in which he won both the Masters Tournament and the British Open Championship was easily the zenith of his career.

Zephyr

A strong, chilly wind, like the sustained gusts that whip across the United Kingdom and bend over flagsticks in Scotland and Ireland.

Zestful

A player who exhibits colorful gestures or animated actions has a zestful nature. Sergio Garcia is a good example of a zestful player while some of the TOUR players appear to compete in a more robotic and expressionless fashion. A zestful player, like Lee Trevino, can be difficult to beat because of their spirited style.

Zodiacally

When events in a tournament consistently occur in favor of a certain player, the success of that player seems "written in the stars," and it is as if he is zodiacally destined to win.

Zombie

A player who has lost a lead or been surprised by the loss of a hole in match play can often wander the course as might a zombie, with an expressionless look of shock on his face.

Zone

When a player is "in the zone," he is playing beyond his normal level of skill and outside his normal level of consciousness. Everything seems to come easy to the player who is in the zone. Fairways look like runways, confidence runs high, and the cups appear to be the size of washtubs. The swing mechanics require no thought, and everything just "clicks."

Zoophagous

A gritty, hungry player with a predatory attitude and a voracious appetite for victory can never be counted out. Lee Trevino and Tiger Woods are two such carnivorous-type competitors.

Zygote

Technically, an incipient organ, but when a young player has the germ or skill and the nucleus of talent, he is a TOUR zygote.